DASH DIET COOKBOOK FOR TWO

200 Healthy Low-Sodium simple Recipes to help you lower your Blood Pressure.
7 - week plan and Meal Prep 2021 to boost your immune system and lose weight

Jennifer Larsen

Copyright - 2021 - by Jennifer Larsen

All rights reserved.

The content contained within this book may not be reproduced, duplicated or transmitted without direct written permission from the author or the publisher.

Under no circumstances will any blame or legal responsibility be held against the publisher, or author, for any damages, reparation, or monetary loss due to the information contained within this book. Either directly or indirectly.

Legal Notice:

This book is copyright protected. This book is only for personal use. You cannot amend, distribute, sell, use, quote or paraphrase any part, or the content within this book, without the consent of the author or publisher.

Disclaimer Notice:

Please note the information contained within this document is for educational and entertainment purposes only. All effort has been executed to present accurate, up to date, and reliable, complete information. No warranties of any kind are declared or implied. Readers acknowledge that the author is not engaging in the rendering of legal, financial, medical or professional advice. The content within this book has been derived from various sources. Please consult a licensed professional before attempting any techniques outlined in this book.

By reading this document, the reader agrees that under no circumstances is the author responsible for any losses, direct or indirect, which are incurred as a result of the use of information contained within this document, including, but not limited to, - errors, omissions, or inaccuracies.

Table of Contents

INTRODUCTION   15

CHAPTER 1. STEP BY STEP PLAN TO PREPARE YOUR METABOLISM   17

Step 1 - Determine Your Calorie Target   17

Step 2 - Identify the Dash Diet Ideal for Your Calorie Target   17

Step 3 - Ready to Dash   18

Shopping list   18

CHAPTER 2. 1 WEEK PLAN TO RESET YOUR METABOLISM AND BOOST YOUR IMMUNE SYSTEM   23

Breakfast   25

1. Veggie Toasts   26

2. Special Sausage   27

3. Cod with Pearl Onions   28

4. Lemon Sole and Swiss Chard   29

5. Snapper Fillets and Veggies   30

6. Delicious Red Snapper   31

7. Air Fried Branzino   32

8. Spanish Salmon   33

9. Salmon and Avocado Salad   34

Lunch   35

10. Spicy Bean Chili   36

11. Sesame Ginger Chicken Stir-Fry With Cauliflower Rice   37

12. Spinach, Mushroom, And Feta Cheese Scramble   38

13. Roasted Tofu & Peanut Noodle Salad	39
14. Tomato And Green Soup	40
15. Hawaiian Salmon	41
16. Marinated Salmon	42
17. Sesame Chicken Salad	43
18. Coconut Chicken Tenders	44
19. Mushroom Scrambled Eggs	45
Dinner	**47**
20. French Country Chicken	48
21. Beef Stroganoff	49
22. Chipotle Spiced Shrimp	50
23. Pizza Margherita	51
24. Citrus Salad	52
25. Roasted Salmon With Maple Glaze	53
26. Garlic Mashed Potatoes	54
27. Tomato- Bean Soup with Breadsticks	55
28. Blackened Chicken with Berry Salad	56
Snacks	**57**
29. Cajun Popcorn	58
30. Lime Tortilla Chips	59
31. Peach Salsa	60
32. Vegetable Chips	61
33. DASH Devilled Eggs	62

34. Vanilla Lemon Parfait	63
35. Figs with Goat Cheese	64
CHAPTER 3. 2 WEEKS METABOLISM-BOOSTING MENU	**65**

Breakfast 67

36. No-Bake Breakfast Granola Bars	68
37. Banana and Peanut Butter Breakfast Smoothie	69
38. Apple-Spice Baked Oatmeal	70
39. Banana-Nut Pancakes	71
40. Cheese and Broccoli Mini Egg Omelets	72
41. Mushroom and Shallot Frittata	73
42. Green Breakfast Smoothie	74
43. Fruit and Grain Breakfast	75
44. Perfect Granola	76
45. Blueberry Oat Pancakes	77

Lunch 79

46. Steak Tacos	80
47. Pasta With Spinach, Garbanzos, And Raisins	81
48. Mango salsa pizza	82
49. Stuffed Eggplant	83
50. Acorn Squash With Apples	84
51. Broiled white sea bass	85
52. Chicken Alfredo with Whole-Wheat Bowtie Pasta	86
53. Broccoli, garlic, and rigatoni	87

54. Spinach Mushroom Frittata — 88

Dinner — 89

55. Avocado Cucumber Soup — 90
56. Whole Grain Bruschetta — 91
57. Russian Cold Soup — 92
58. Greek Feta Salad — 93
59. Olive Pesto — 94
60. Mackerel Tapas — 95
61. Orange N Chicory Salad — 96
62. Fruity Lamb's Lettuce — 97
63. Bell Pepper Mackerel — 98

Snack — 99

64. Pineapple Sundae — 100
65. Peach Parfait — 101
66. PBA Sandwich — 102
67. Iced Espresso Latte — 103
68. Minty-Lime Iced Tea — 104
69. Fruit Smoothies — 105
70. Berry Smoothie — 106

CHAPTER 4. 30 DAYS DASH MEAL PREPARATION PLANS 2021 — 107

Breakfast — 111

71. Bacon Egg & Spinach Casserole — 112
72. Biscuits and Gravy — 113

73. Breakfast Tostada	114
74. Creamy Banana Oatmeal	115
75. Egg Salad	116
76. Homemade Bacon	117
77. Oatmeal Pancakes	118
78. Sausage and Potatoes Mix	119
79. Nice Wheat Muffins	120
80. Pumpkin Vanilla Smoothie	121
81. Pumpkin Pie Smoothie Delight	122
82. Buckwheat Pancakes with Strawberries	123
83. Triple Muffins	124
84. Pineapple Potato Salad	125
85. Breakfast Sausage Gravy	126
86. Bisquick Turkey Breakfast Balls	127
87. Easy Omelet Waffles	128
88. Breakfast Fruit Bowl	129
Lunch	**131**
89. Curried Chicken wrap	132
90. Open-Faced Garden Tuna Sandwich	133
91. Baked Macaroni	134
92. Zucchini Pad Thai	135
93. Easy Roasted Salmon	136
94. Shrimp with Pasta, Artichoke, and Spinach	137
95. Pistachio Crusted Halibut with Spicy Yogurt	138

96. Paella with Chicken, Leeks, and Tarragon	139
97. Roasted Brussels Sprouts, Chicken, and Potatoes	140
98. Shepherd's Pie	141
99. Salmon and Edamame Cakes	142
100. Flat Bread Pizza	143
101. Spinach Salad with Walnuts and Strawberry	144
102. Chicken Vegetable Soup	145
103. Avocado Sandwich with Lemon and Cilantro	146
104. Tofu and Mushroom Burger	147
105. Cobb Salad	148
106. Veggie Sushi	149

Dinner — 151

107. Turkey Stir Fry with Vegetables	152
108. Tuscan White Beans with Shrimp, Spinach, and Feta	153
109. Chicken & Broccoli in Sesame Noodles	154
110. Spicy Baked Potatoes	155
111. Tandoori Chicken	156
112. Pork Tenderloin with Sweet Potatoes & Apple	157
113. Tasty Tortilla Bake	158
114. Pear Quesadillas	159
115. Porcini Mushrooms With Pasta	160
116. Shrimp & Nectarine Salad	161
117. Pork Chops with Tomato Curry	162

118. Thai Chicken Pasta Skillet	163
119. Chili-Lime Grilled Pineapple	164
120. Peppered Sole	165
121. Shrimp Orzo with Feta	166
122. Beef and Blue Cheese Penne with Pesto	167
123. California Quinoa	168
124. Peppered Tuna Kabobs	169

Snack

	171
125. Mini Bell Pepper Loaded Nachos	172
126. Zucchini Pizza Boats	173
127. Fruit Skewers with Vanilla Honey Yogurt Dip	174
128. Baked Parmesan Zucchini Sticks	175
129. Spinach Artichoke Dip	176
130. Buffalo Chickpea and Artichoke Taquitos	177
131. Loaded Avocado Quesadillas	178
132. Crunchy Kale Chips	179
133. Crispy Parmesan Ranch Zucchini Chips	180
134. Cinnamon Yogurt Fruit Dip	181
135. Chocolate Yogurt Pudding	182
136. Peanut Butter Energy Bites	183
137. Apple Pie Oat Bars	184
138. Baked Chicken Nuggets	185
139. Cinnamon Apples	186

140. Ranch and Cheese Bell Pepper Poppers	187
141. Baked Chicken Tacos	188
142. Sweet and Spicy Roasted Sweet Potato Rounds	189

Dessert   191

143. Easy Brownies	192
144. Vanilla Black Bean Brownies	193
145. Apple Tart	194
146. Chocolate Cake	195
147. Banana Cake	196
148. Apple Cupcakes	197
149. Easy Fudge	198
150. Fruit Salad	199
151. Rhubarb Pie	200
152. Blueberry Curd	201
153. Coconut Mousse	202
154. Easy Chocolate Pudding	203
155. Blueberry Orange Compote	204
156. Vanilla Apple Mix	205
157. Nigella Mango Mix	206
158. Almond Peach Mix	207
159. Easy Lemon Cream	208
160. Vanilla Pumpkin Bars	209

CHAPTER 5. DASH DIET HEALTHY RECIPES FOR BEGINNERS — 211

Breakfast — 211

161. Buckwheat Crepes — 212
162. Pumpkin Granola Yogurt Parfait — 213
163. Sweet Potato Oat Waffles — 214
164. French Toast — 215
165. Open Face Breakfast Sandwich — 216
166. Potato salad Side dish — 217
167. Broccoli With Garlic And Lemon — 218
168. Cauliflower Mashed Potatoes — 219
169. Green Beans With Red Pepper & Garlic — 220
170. Honey Sage Carrots — 221

Salads — 223

171. Chicken Salad — 224
172. Asian Veggie Salad with Snow Peas — 225
173. Baked Cod with a Citrus Twist — 226
174. The Mighty Tabbouleh Salad — 227
175. Greek Salad with Feta Crumbles — 228

Soups — 229

176. Zucchini Soup — 230
177. Creamy Pumpkin Soup — 231
178. Home Made Tomato Soup — 232
179. Savory Tomato Lentil Soup — 233

180. Creamy Butternut Squash Soup	234
Vegan and Vegetarian	**235**
181. Tomatoes, Asparagus and Goat Cheese Penne	236
182. Garden Quesadillas	237
183. Bean Barley Burgers	238
184. Southwestern Vegetables Taco	239
185. Rotelle Pasta with Sun-Dried Tomato and Black Olive Sauce	240
Fish and Seafood	**241**
186. Scallop & Veg Skewers	242
187. Honey Scallops	243
188. Red Onion Salmon	244
189. Halibut in a Spiced Salsa	245
190. Halibut with a Pea Puree	246
Poultry & Meat	**247**
191. Breaded And Baked Chicken Tenders	248
192. Savory Pork Loin	249
193. Honey-Garlic Pork Chops	250
194. Beef Tenderloin Medallions With Horseradish Yogurt Sauce	251
195. Greek-Style Top Round Steaks	252
Desserts	**253**
196. Apricot & Almond Crisp	254
197. Fresh Strawberries With Yoghurt And Honey	255
198. Fruit & Nut Bar	256

199. Milk Chocolate Pudding   257

200. Orange Dream Smoothie   258

CONCLUSION   **259**

INTRODUCTION

Dash Diet was known for many years now, but it has only recently gained widespread attention. It was initially created by the National Heart Lung and Blood Institute to deal with raised blood pressure. In time, it evolved into a weight loss plan as well.

The diet's full name is Dietary Approaches to Stop Hypertension. It is a low-calorie diet used to lowering blood pressure and improving your cardiovascular health.

It was designed for people who have raised blood pressure. You can still use this diet even if your blood pressure is within acceptable limits and you want to lose weight but do not want to lose muscle.

The DASH is a very balanced diet created based on National Dietary Recommendations. This is low fat, low sodium, and low cholesterol diet rich in fiber, potassium, and magnesium; all ingredients are proven to be useful in lowering blood pressure.

The DASH diet is a very simple concept. You will not have to give up many of the foods you already like; it is very easy to fit into your daily routine, and you can eat without any side effects. What makes this diet different from others is that it is a healthy diet that has been initially created and tested for a specific purpose to be very effective in reducing blood pressure.

The diet is very balanced, and you will choose from a wide variety of foods. The DASH diet principles are rich in vegetables, fruits, whole grains, and fat-free or low-fat dairy products. The diet is also rich in omega-3 fatty acids.

The DASH diet is so effective because it is much more than only limited to blood pressure-lowering and has been proven to be an extremely successful weight loss plan.

When you are following this diet, the goal is to cut down on sodium, cholesterol, and 'bad' fats; hence, it is something that anyone can use, no matter where you are at in your weight loss journey. This diet is very easy to implement, but the following tips can also help you out.

Be sure to cut down on high-fat dairy products- this can be found in milk, ice cream, and cheese and eat more high fiber foods so that you will easily feel fuller, and therefore you will be able to eat less. Be sure to eat colorful vegetables and foods high in fiber, like vegetables- this should be done every day.

Eat a good amount of fish- this is something that is easy to do and can easily be incorporated into your daily diet. Fish is very healthy and is loaded with many good nutrients.

Try to limit salt and sugar intake- they add to the general cost of your shopping. Look for products with less sodium and sugar.

This diet will help you to lose weight, and it has no known side effects. This is why, in time, the DASH diet started to gain popularity. It is a simple and easy diet that does work and is a good choice for weight loss, but it does not want to lose muscle.

The DASH diet is not about cutting down on calories; it is a diet that includes many simple, everyday foods that you will be able to use easily in your daily routine. This is a healthy diet based on a specific goal.

CHAPTER 1. STEP BY STEP PLAN TO PREPARE YOUR METABOLISM

According to the dash diet plan, you need around 4 portions of vegetables, 4 portions of fruits, and 2-3 portions of low-fat dairy items. If you compare these portions with those of an American's average diet, you'll see that the latter contains only one or less portion of dairy and 3-4 portions of fruits and vegetables. You should also consume poultry, fish, and nuts. You need to limit red meat, sugary foods, beverages, and fatty foods for these nutritious foods.

Eat this balanced diet of nutritious, healthful foods for 14 days, and you'll see obvious differences in your blood pressure readings, and overall health. If your blood pressure is "mildly" high, it will decrease to a level where your doctor might advise you to go off your medication. Stick to the dash diet to avail of the main other mental and physical health benefits.

Dash in Simple Steps

Understanding how to implement the dash plan is as simple as three easy steps. So, let's get started.

Step 1 – Determine Your Calorie Target

Every individual has different energy requirements. A 120-pound senior citizen's energy needs are different from those of a 160-pound football player.

When practicing a dash, you should take the first step to determine the number of calories you should get every day. Once calculated easily on line, you can determine which type of dash diet you should consume.

Step 2 – Identify the Dash Diet Ideal for Your Calorie Target

You already know what your necessary calorie intake is dash diet can give you efficient results. This will further help you decide the number of portions you need from every food group to stay healthy and active.

Step 3 – Ready to Dash

The following steps are as important as controlling high blood pressure to use the dash the right way.

- Discuss your diet plan with your physician and have them analyze your blood pressure readings.

- Mark the day when you intend to start the dash eating plan on your calendar.

- Inform friends and family that you are practicing the dash diet as they can support you in your endeavors.

- Get rid of all food products that are not a part of the dash diet plan, especially chips, candy bars, ice cream, and other snacks.

- Change your habits. Don't eat in front of the television. Have physical activity as part of your daily routine.

Shopping List

Fruits

Tangy, sweet, soft, crunchy, tine, huge; fruits are one such unique food group that offers a huge variety to tantalize your taste buds and keep you healthy and fit. Forming a beneficial constituent of the dash diet, they are the easiest to prepare. They are an important source of minerals, magnesium, potassium, fiber, and other nutrients. Fruits are generally low in fat, excluding coconuts and avocados.

According to the dash diet, you should eat fruits in great quantities than an average American. If you're not a fruit fan, then fruit juice can also come in handy. Read the product label to ensure it is 100 percent fruit juice because only then you'll get real juice nutrition. Avoid consuming drinks, labeled fruit cocktails, or fruit drinks as they usually have added sugars and can increase your calorie intake.

Your daily diet should include at least 4 to 5 servings of fruits. A single serving includes:

- One medium-sized or a half cup of fruit

- Half cup of pure fruit juice

Vegetables

Have you ever eaten any Italian food that doesn't have tomato sauce? Or Chinese food that doesn't have broccoli and onions? Vegetables give a special color, texture, and of course, taste to your favorite cuisines. Rich nutrients, including potassium, fiber, magnesium, vegetables are low in fat, sodium, and calories, and that's why they are a key element of the dash diet.

Your daily diet should include at least 4 to 5 servings of vegetables. A single serving includes:

- Half cup of cooked vegetable, such as broccoli, kale, spinach, cauliflower, etc.
- One cup of fresh leafy vegetables, such as lettuce or spinach
- Three-fourth cup of vegetable juice
- Half potato or 1/4 cup of mashed potato
- Half cup of tomato sauce

Dairy Foods

Though dairy products have been a vital part of our daily diet since the old days, the dash diet further emphasizes their importance as they are a great source of protein, calcium, and vitamin D. Still, you need to remember that they can be high in saturated fat, so it is always good to choose nonfat or low-fat dairy products. This will give you enormous health benefits without making additions to your fat consumption.

Your daily diet should have at least 3 servings of dairy products. A single serving includes:

- One cup of 2 percent low-fat milk, 1 percent low-fat milk, or skim milk
- 1/3 cup of nonfat milk powder
- One cup of low-fat or nonfat cottage cheese
- One cup of nonfat or low-fat yogurt
- Half cup of nonfat or low-fat frozen yogurt
- 1/4 cups of nonfat or low-fat cheeses, such as ricotta and cheddar

Grains

We mean everything from bread, cereals, pasta, rice, bagels, and tortillas by grains.

Your daily diet should have at least 6 servings of grain. A single serving includes:

- One slice of whole wheat bread
- 1/4 cup dry cereal
- Half cup cooked pasta, rice, or cereal

Poultry, Lean Meat and Fish

Meat is a great source of vitamins B, protein, zinc, and iron. However, even lean meats contain huge amounts of cholesterol and fat, so it is better not to make them your diet's mainstay. While following the dash diet plan, you can reduce regular meat portions and replace them with vegetables and fruits.

Your diet should have at least 5 servings of lean meat, fish, and poultry. A single serving includes:

- 1/4 cup cooked seafood, lean meat, or skinless poultry
- One egg

Sweets and Desserts

The dash diet doesn't let you crave those tempting, sweet-smelling desserts that you can't live without. You don't need to banish them at all. Instead, consume them in limited amounts.

You should have 4 or fewer servings of sweets and desserts every week. A single serving includes:

- One tbsp. sugar, jam, or jelly
- Half cup sorbet
- One cup lemonade

Legumes, Nuts, and Seeds

This is an important food group of the dash diet as it offers you some delicious and healthy choices. Having lentils, peas, almonds, kidney beans, sunflower seeds, and many other healthful foods, this family supports your physical and mental health with protein, potassium, magnesium, and fiber. Furthermore, they are a rich source of phytochemicals. These plant-based compounds keep you protected from cardiovascular diseases and certain types of cancer.

Since these foods have greater amounts of calories, they should be consumed in limited quantities.

Legumes, nuts, and seeds should be consumed at least 4 times a week. A single serving includes:

- 1/3 cup nuts
- Half cup cooked peas or beans
- Two tbsps. seeds

Fats and Oils

Wonder why is this food family a part of the dash diet? Well, your body needs some fats and oils to absorb vitamins and keep your immune system strong. However, excessive fat consumption can increase your chances of developing diabetes, obesity, and heart disease.

The dash diet maintains a healthy balance and restricts total fat to less than 27 percent of daily calories. Moreover, it focuses on the consumption of monosaturated fats.

Your daily diet should include at least 2 servings of oils and fats. A single service includes:

- Two tbsps. salad dressing
- One tbsp. mayonnaise
- One tsp. soft margarine

CHAPTER 2. 1 WEEK PLAN TO RESET YOUR METABOLISM AND BOOST YOUR IMMUNE SYSTEM

DAY	BREAKFAST	LUNCH	DINNER	SNACK
1	VEGGIE TOAST	SESAME GINGER CHICKEN STIR-FRY WITH CAULIFLOWER RICE	FRENCH COUNTRY CHICKEN	PEACH SALSA
2	DELICIOUS RED SNAPPER	TOMATO AND GREEN SOUP	PIZZA MARGHERITA	VEGETABLE CHIPS
3	SPECIAL SAUSAGE	MUSHROOM SCRAMBLED EGG	CITRUS SALAD	CAJUN POPCORN
4	SPANISH SALMON	SPINACH, MUSHROOM, AND FETA CHEESE SCRAMBLE	BLACKENED CHICKEN WITH BERRY SALAD	LIME TORTILLA CHIPS
5	COD WITH PEAR ONIONS	SESAME CHICKEN SALAD	GARLIC MASHED POTATOES	VANILLA LEMON PARFAIT
6	SALMON AND AVOCADO SALAD	HAWAIIAN SALMON	TOMATO-BEAN SOUP WITH BREADSTICKS	DASH DEVILLED EGGS
7	AIR FRIED BRANZINO	ROASTED TOFU & PEANUT NOODLE SALAD	CHIPOTLE SPICED SHRIMP	FIGS WITH GOAT CHEESE

BREAKFAST

1. VEGGIE TOASTS

PREPARATION TIME
10 MIN

COOKING TIME
15 MIN

SERVINGS
2

INGREDIENTS:
- 1 red bell pepper
- 1 cup cremini mushrooms; sliced
- 4 bread slices
- 2 tbsp. butter; soft
- 1 yellow squash; chopped.
- 2 green onions; sliced
- 1 tbsp. olive oil
- 1/2 cup goat cheese; crumbled

DIRECTIONS:

Cut red bell pepper into thin strips

Mix red bell pepper with mushrooms, squash, green onions, and oil, toss in a bowl.

Move to your air fryer and cook them at a temperature of 350°F for about 10 minutes.

Shake the fryer once and transfer them into a bowl.

Spread butter on bread slices, then introduce them to your air fryer and cook them at a temperature of 350°F.

Cook for about 5 minutes.

Cut the veggie mix on each bread slice.

Use crumbled cheese as toppings

Nutrition: Calories: 112 Total Fat: 1.58g Total Carbohydrates: 21g Fiber: 1g Sugar: 2g Protein: 3g

2. SPECIAL SAUSAGE

 **PREPARATION TIME** 10 MIN

 **COOKING TIME** 10 MIN

 **SERVINGS** 2

INGREDIENTS:
- 1 lb. sausages; sliced
- 1 red bell pepper; cut into strips
- 1/2 cup yellow onion; chopped.
- 1/2 cup chicken stock
- 1/3 cup ketchup
- 3 tbsp. brown sugar
- 2 tbsp. mustard
- 2 tbsp. apple cider vinegar

DIRECTIONS:

Mix sugar with ketchup, mustard, stock, and vinegar in a clean bowl and whisk well.

Mix sausage slices with bell pepper, onion, and sweet and sour mix in your fryer's pan.

Then toss and cook at a temperature of 350 °F for 10 minutes.

Divide into different bowls and serve.

Nutrition: Calories: 191 Total Fat: 10g Total Carbohydrates: 14g Fiber: 4g Sugar: 7g Protein: 13g

3. COD WITH PEARL ONIONS

PREPARATION TIME
10 MIN

COOKING TIME
15 MIN

SERVINGS
2

INGREDIENTS:

- 14 ounces pearl onions 2 medium cod fillets
- 1 tablespoon parsley, dried
- 1 teaspoon thyme
- Black dried pepper to the taste
- 8 ounces mushrooms, sliced

DIRECTIONS:

Put fish in a heatproof dish that fits your air fryer, add onions, parsley, mushrooms, thyme, and black pepper.

Toss well to coat, place in your air fryer, cook at a temperature of 350 degrees F and cook for 15 minutes.

Divide all of it into different plates and serve immediately.

Serve and enjoy.

Nutrition: Calories: 178 Total Fat: 1.8g Total Carbohydrates: 15.8g Fiber: 1.5g Sugar: 0g Protein: 22.9g

4. LEMON SOLE AND SWISS CHARD

PREPARATION TIME
10 MIN

COOKING TIME
14 MIN

SERVINGS
2

INGREDIENTS:

- 1 teaspoon lemon zest, grated
- 4 white bread slices, quartered
- 1/4cup walnuts, chopped
- 1/4cup parmesan, grated
- 4 tablespoons olive oil
- 4 sole fillets, boneless
- Salt and black pepper to the taste
- 4 tablespoons butter
- 1/4cup lemon juice
- 3 tablespoons capers
- 2 garlic cloves, minced
- 2 bunches Swiss chard, chopped

DIRECTIONS:

Mix the bread with walnuts, cheese, and lemon zest in a food processor and pulse well.

Add about half of the olive oil, and pulse well again.

Keep it aside for a while.

Heat the pan with the butter over medium heat, and add lemon juice, salt, pepper, and capers.

Stir gently and add fish and toss it. Move the fish to your preheated air fryer's basket.

Top with some bread mix you already made at the start.

Cook at 350 degrees F for 14 minutes.

Also, heat another pan containing the remaining oil, then add garlic, Swiss chard, salt, and pepper.

Stir the resulting mixture gently, cook for about 2 minutes and remove the heat.

Divide fish into different plates

Serve with sautéed chard on the side.

Enjoy!

Nutrition: Calories: 160 Total Fat: 3g Total Carbohydrates: 4g Fiber: 1g Sugar: 1g Protein: 29g

5. SNAPPER FILLETS AND VEGGIES

PREPARATION TIME
10 MIN

COOKING TIME
14 MIN

SERVINGS
2

INGREDIENTS:

- 2 red snapper fillets, boneless
- 1 tablespoon olive oil
- 1/2 cup red bell pepper, chopped
- 1/2 cup green bell pepper, chopped
- 1/2 cup leeks, chopped
- Salt and black pepper to the taste
- 1 teaspoon tarragon, dried
- A splash of white wine

DIRECTIONS:

Cut red bell pepper into thin strips

Mix red bell pepper with mushrooms, squash, green onions, and oil, toss in a bowl.

Move to your air fryer and cook them at a temperature of 350°F for about 10 minutes.

Shake the fryer once and transfer them into a bowl.

Spread butter on bread slices, then introduce them to your air fryer and cook them at a temperature of 350°F.

Cook for about 5 minutes.

Cut the veggie mix on each bread slice.

Use crumbled cheese as toppings

Nutrition: Calories: 340 Total Fat: 11g Total Carbohydrates: 26g Fiber: 3g Sugar: 3g Protein: 37g

6. DELICIOUS RED SNAPPER

 **PREPARATION TIME**
30 MIN

 **COOKING TIME**
15 MIN

 **SERVINGS**
2

INGREDIENTS:

- 1 big red snapper, cleaned and scored Salt and black pepper to the taste
- 3 garlic cloves, minced
- 1 jalapeno, chopped
- 1/4-pound okra, chopped
- 1 tablespoon butter
- 2 tablespoons olive oil
- 1 red bell pepper, chopped
- 2 tablespoons white wine
- 2 tablespoons parsley, chopped

DIRECTIONS:

Mix the jalapeno, wine with garlic, stir well and rub snapper with this mix.

Flavor the fish with salt and pepper in a bowl and keep it aside for 30 minutes.

Also, add heat to a pan with about 1 tablespoon of butter over medium heat.

Then add bell pepper and okra.

Stir the resulting mixture gently and cook for 5 minutes.

Stuff red snapper's belly with this mix, also add parsley and rub with the olive oil.

Place in a preheated air fryer and cook at a temperature of 400 degrees F for 15 minutes. Flip the fish halfway while cooking.

Divide into different plates and serve.

Enjoy!

Nutrition: Calories: 145 Total Fat: 2g Total Carbohydrates: 0g Fiber: 0g Sugar: 0g Protein: 29g

7. AIR FRIED BRANZINO

PREPARATION TIME
10 MIN

COOKING TIME
10 MIN

SERVINGS
2

INGREDIENTS:

- Zest from 1 lemon, grated
- Zest from 1 orange, grated
- Juice from 1/2 lemon
- Juice from 1/2 orange
- Salt and black pepper to the taste
- 4 medium branzino fillets, boneless
- 1/2 cup parsley, chopped
- 2 tablespoons olive oil
- A pinch of red pepper flakes, crushed

DIRECTIONS:

Mix the fish fillets with lemon zest, orange zest, lemon juice, orange juice, salt, pepper, oil, and pepper flakes in a clean and large bowl.

Toss perfectly and move the fillets to an air fryer preheated at 350 degrees F

Bake for 10 minutes, flipping fillets once.

Divide fish into different plates, sprinkle with parsley, and serve immediately.

Enjoy!

Nutrition: Calories: 228 Total Fat: 17g Total Carbohydrates: 0g Fiber: 0g Sugar: 0g Protein: 17g

 **PREPARATION TIME**
10 MIN

 **COOKING TIME**
15 MIN

 **SERVINGS**
2

8. SPANISH SALMON

INGREDIENTS:

- 2 cups bread croutons
- 3 red onions, cut into medium wedges
- 3/4 cup green olives, pitted
- 3 red bell peppers, cut into medium wedges
- 1/2 teaspoon smoked paprika
- Salt and black pepper to the taste
- 5 tablespoons olive oil
- 6 medium salmon fillets, skinless and boneless 2 tablespoons parsley, chopped

DIRECTIONS:

Mix bread croutons with onion wedges, bell pepper ones, olives, salt, pepper, paprika, and 3 tablespoons olive oil in a heatproof dish that fits your air fryer.

Toss well to coat and place in your air fryer

Cook at a temperature of 356 degrees F for 7 minutes.

Rub salmon with the rest of the oil, add over veggies, and cook at 360 degrees F for 8 minutes.

Divide fish and veggie mix into different plates, sprinkle parsley all over, and serve.

Enjoy!

Nutrition: Calories: 133 Total Fat: 1g Total Carbohydrates: 2g Fiber: 0g Sugar: 0g Protein: 28g

9. SALMON AND AVOCADO SALAD

PREPARATION TIME
10 MIN

COOKING TIME
20 MIN

SERVINGS
2

INGREDIENTS:

- 2 medium salmon fillets
- 1/4cup melted butter
- 4 ounces mushrooms, sliced
- Sea salt and black pepper to the taste
- 12 cherry tomatoes, halved
- 2 tablespoons olive oil
- 8 ounces lettuce leaves, torn
- 1 avocado, pitted, peeled and cubed
- 1 jalapeno pepper, chopped
- 5 cilantro springs, chopped
- 2 tablespoons white wine vinegar
- 1-ounce feta cheese, crumbled

DIRECTIONS:

Place the salmon neatly on a lined baking sheet, then brush all over with 2 tablespoons melted butter.

Put some salt and pepper as seasoning.

Broil for about 15 minutes over medium heat and then keep warm.

Also, add heat to a pan containing the remaining butter over medium heat.

Add mushrooms and stir gently. Cook for some minutes.

Prepare the tomatoes in a bowl, put salt, pepper and 1 tablespoon olive oil, then toss to coat.

Mix salmon with mushrooms, lettuce, avocado, tomatoes, jalapeno, and cilantro in a salad bowl.

Add the remaining oil, vinegar, salt and pepper.

Finally, sprinkle cheese on top and serve. Enjoy!

Nutrition: Calories: 297 Total Fat: 20g Total Carbohydrates: 14g Fiber: 4g Sugar: 5g Protein: 21g

LUNCH

10. SPICY BEAN CHILI

PREPARATION TIME
15 MIN

COOKING TIME
20 MIN

SERVINGS
2

INGREDIENTS:

- 1 teaspoon of Grapeseed Oil
- 1/2 Medium size Red Onion
- 1/2 Jalapeno Pepper
- 1 Garlic Clove
- 15 oz of low sodium Red Kidney Beans
- 3/4 cup of vegetable broth (low sodium)
- 1/2 cup crushed tomatoes (canned)
- 3/4 teaspoon chili powder
- 1/4 teaspoon of sea salt
- 1/8 teaspoon of ground cinnamon

DIRECTIONS:

Warm oil in a saucepan with medium-high heat.

Add the onion and jalapeño, after which you sauté for 5 minutes till the onion is caramelized.

Put the garlic and sauté until fragrant for about 30 seconds.

Add the rest of the ingredients and stir. Allow them to a boil 1 minute warmly. Cover with the lid and simmer in medium heat for 10 minutes until well combined.

Garnish as you like with either quark and fresh coriander or organic low-fat sour cream

Nutrition: Calories: 270 Total Fat: 2g Total Carbohydrates: 45g Fiber: 17g Sugar: 5g Protein: 17g

11. SESAME GINGER CHICKEN STIR-FRY WITH CAULIFLOWER RICE

PREPARATION TIME 20 MIN

COOKING TIME 20 MIN

SERVINGS 2

INGREDIENTS:

For Cauliflower Rice
- 1 small head of cauliflower
- 2 tablespoons chicken bone bread
- 1/4 teaspoon sea salt
- 1 tablespoon of coconut oil

For sesame ginger chicken stir
- 1 1/2 cups Original chicken bone bread
- 2 tablespoon tapioca starch
- 1 Lb. boneless chicken breasts, chopped
- 1 medium red bell pepper, chopped
- 1/4 teaspoon Organic Crushed Red Pepper
- 1 tablespoon of coconut oil
- 3 cloves garlic, minced
- 1 tablespoon grated fresh ginger
- 1/2 teaspoon sea salt
- 1-pound asparagus, chopped
- 4 ounces shiitake mushrooms, chopped
- 2 tablespoons organic Toasted Sesame Seeds

DIRECTIONS:

Using a food processor, pulse the cauliflower head in batches until the rice texture is good enough for cauliflower rice.

Put the coconut oil in a skillet on medium-high heat and add the cauliflower; cook for 2 minutes and stir.

Stir in the bone broth and sea salt and cook for the next 5 minutes until soft. Set aside.

Mix tapioca, bone broth, and crushed red pepper till they are smooth, set it aside. Place a large skillet on medium-high heat and add coconut oil.

Put the chicken and fry for 5 minutes to become crispy. Take off the skillet. Stir into the skillet onions, ginger, garlic, and salt, and cook for 3 minutes.

Stir in the mixture of bone broth and stir continuously for 2 minutes over medium heat until thickened. Add the chicken; stir fry to melt well. Sprinkle them with sesame seeds.

Serve it with Rice Cauliflower.

Nutrition: Calories: 225 Total Fat: 5g Total Carbohydrates: 23g Fiber: 1g Sugar: 10g Protein: 25g

12. SPINACH, MUSHROOM, AND FETA CHEESE SCRAMBLE

PREPARATION TIME 5 MIN

COOKING TIME 10 MIN

SERVINGS 2

INGREDIENTS:

- 1 cup fresh spinach, diced
- 1 whole egg
- Cooking spray
- 1/2 cup fresh mushrooms, sliced
- 2 tablespoons feta cheese
- Pepper to taste.

DIRECTIONS:

Get and place a nonstick frying pan over medium heat. Spray with cooking spray.

Add spinach and mushrooms and cook for 2-3 minutes to wilt the mushrooms

Break the raw egg into a bowl, add feta cheese and pepper, and whisk.

Add the mixture into the saucepan containing the vegetables.

Cook for another 3-4 minutes and stir continuously until the eggs are cooked well.

Nutrition: Calories: 194 Total Fat: 11g Total Carbohydrates: 4g Fiber: 0.8g Sugar: 0.7g Protein: 22g

13. ROASTED TOFU & PEANUT NOODLE SALAD

- **PREPARATION TIME** 10 MIN
- **COOKING TIME** 30 MIN
- **SERVINGS** 2

INGREDIENTS:

- 6 ounces whole spaghetti
- 1/2 cup of smooth, natural peanut butter
- 1/4 cup of lime juice
- 1/4 cup of soy sauce
- 1 tablespoon of canola oil
- 16-ounce extra firm water-tofu, sliced into 1/2-inch cubes
- 1 tablespoon of fresh ginger
- 6 cups of thinly sliced Napa cabbage
- 1 medium orange pepper, thinly sliced
- 3 tablespoons of water
- 3 cloves of garlic, minced
- 1 cup of thinly sloped pepper

DIRECTIONS:

Prepare the oven to 450 degrees F and coat the baking sheet with cooking spray.

Put the spaghetti in a big pot of water and bring it to a boil.

Add the lime juice, oil, and soy sauce in a cup and mix properly. Add the tofu to the mixture and marinate for 10 minutes. Stir continuously.

Using a slotted spoon, transfer the tofu to the baking sheet, and conserve the marinade. Allow the tofu to roast for 16-18 minutes until golden brown. Stir only once halfway.

Put the spaghetti in a pot and cook as described in the packet. Drain and set aside

Into the conserved marinade, whisk 3 tablespoons of sugar, garlic, peanut butter, and ginger.

Stir in the pasta, snow peas, salmon, pepper bell, and mix. Top with the tofu.

Nutrition: Calories: 423 Total Fat: 21g Total Carbohydrates: 42g Fiber: 8g Sugar: 0g Protein: 21g

14. TOMATO AND GREEN SOUP

PREPARATION TIME 5 MIN

COOKING TIME 30 MIN

SERVINGS 2

INGREDIENTS:

- 1 cup of chopped onion
- 1 cup of chopped carrots
- 2 teaspoons butter
- 6 cups of reduced-sodium chicken or vegetable broth
- 1 pound of fresh green beans, cut into 1-inch pieces
- 1 garlic clove, chopped
- 3 cups of fresh tomatoes
- 1/4 cup chopped basil or 1 tablespoon of dried basil
- 1/2 teaspoon salt
- 1/4 teaspoon pepper

DIRECTIONS:

Sauté onion and buttered carrots in a wide saucepan for 5 minutes.

Stir in water, garlic, beans, and bring to a boil. Cover and simmer for 20 minutes to make the vegetable tender.

Stir in onions, salt, pepper, and basil to taste.

Cover and cook for another 5 minutes.

Nutrition: Calories: 160 Total Fat: 8g Total Carbohydrates: 2g Fiber: 0g Sugar: 0g Protein: 4g

15. HAWAIIAN SALMON

PREPARATION TIME 10 MIN

COOKING TIME 10 MIN

SERVINGS 2

INGREDIENTS:

- 20 ounces canned pineapple pieces and juice
- 1/2 teaspoon ginger, grated
- 2 teaspoons garlic powder
- 1 teaspoon onion powder
- 1 tablespoon balsamic vinegar
- 2 medium salmon fillets, boneless
- Salt and black pepper to the taste

DIRECTIONS:

Season salmon with garlic powder, onion powder, salt and black pepper. Rub well.

Move to a heatproof dish that fits into your air fryer.

Add ginger and pineapple chunks and toss them gently.

Drizzle the vinegar all over, and place gently in your air fryer and cook at a temperature of 350 degrees F for 10 minutes.

Divide all of it into different plates and serve.

Enjoy!

Nutrition: Calories: 261 Total Fat: 12g Total Carbohydrates: 8g Fiber: 1.3g Sugar: 4g Protein: 29g

16. MARINATED SALMON

PREPARATION TIME 30 MIN

COOKING TIME 20 MIN

SERVINGS 2

INGREDIENTS:

- 1 whole salmon
- 1 tablespoon dill, chopped
- 1 tablespoon tarragon, chopped
- 1 tablespoon garlic, minced
- Juice from 2 lemons
- 1 lemon, sliced
- A pinch of salt and black pepper

DIRECTIONS:

Mix with salt, pepper, and lemon juice in a large fish.

Toss well to coat and keep in the fridge for about an hour.

Stuff the salmon with garlic and lemon slices.

Then introduce to your air fryer's basket and cook at a temperature of 320 degrees F for 25 minutes.

Divide into different plates

Then serve with a tasty coleslaw on the side.

Enjoy!

Nutrition: Calories: 310 Total Fat: 21g Total Carbohydrates: 1g Fiber: 0g Sugar: 0g Protein: 29g

17. SESAME CHICKEN SALAD

PREPARATION TIME
10 MIN

COOKING TIME
12 MIN

SERVINGS
2

INGREDIENTS:

- 1 tablespoon of sesame seeds
- 1 cucumber, peeled, deseeded and sliced
- 100g baby kale, roughly chopped
- 60g Pak choy, finely shredded
- 1/2 red onion, finely sliced
- 20g parsley, chopped
- 150g cooked chicken, shredded

For the dressing:
- 1 tablespoon of extra virgin olive oil
- 1 teaspoon of sesame oil
- 1 lime
- 1 teaspoon of clear honey
- 2 teaspoons of soy sauce

DIRECTIONS:

In a dry frying pan, put the sesame seeds and toast for 2 minutes to become lightly browned and fragrant. Put in a plate and set aside.

Put the olive oil, honey, soy sauce, sesame oil, and lime juice in a small bowl and mix to make the dressing.

Put in a large bowl the kale, cucumber, Pak choy, parsley, and red onion and gently mix. Pour the dressing into the mixture and continue mixing.

Share the salad on two plates topping them with the shredded chicken. Sprinkle the sesame seeds and serve.

Nutrition: Calories: 330 Total Fat: 19g Total Carbohydrates: 13g Fiber: 4g Sugar: 5g Protein: 30g

18. COCONUT CHICKEN TENDERS

PREPARATION TIME
10 MIN

COOKING TIME
25-30 MIN

SERVINGS
2

INGREDIENTS:

- 1/2 cup of almond flour
- 4 pounds of boneless chicken tender
- Salt and pepper
- 4 tablespoons of shredded unsweetened coconut
- 1 teaspoon of garlic powder
- 4 large eggs

DIRECTIONS:

Whisk the eggs very well.

Ready the oven to 300 degrees F. Prepare a baking sheet with parchment paper.

Put the almond flour, garlic powder, and coconut in a dish

Add seasonings, pepper, and salt to the chicken, after which you dip it into the beaten egg

Use the almond flour mixture to dredge the chicken tenders, after which you get it arranged on the baking sheet.

Bake the chicken for 25 minutes until it turns brown and done. Serve hot.

Nutrition: Calories: 136 Total Fat: 8g Total Carbohydrates: 6g Fiber: 0.5g Sugar: 4g Protein: 9g

19. MUSHROOM SCRAMBLED EGGS

PREPARATION TIME
5 MIN

COOKING TIME
6 MIN

SERVINGS
2

INGREDIENTS:

- 2 eggs
- 1 teaspoon ground turmeric
- 1 teaspoon mild curry powder
- 20g kale, roughly chopped
- 1 teaspoon extra virgin olive oil
- 1/2 bird's eye chili, thinly sliced
- a handful of button mushrooms, thinly sliced
- 5g parsley, finely chopped

DIRECTIONS:

Pour turmeric and curry powder in a bowl; add a little water and mix to get a light paste.

Put the kale in a pot and steam for 2–3 minutes.

Pour the oil into a frying pan and heat over medium heat.

Add the chili and mushrooms and fry for 2–3 minutes until they become brown and soft.

Nutrition: Calories: 102 Total Fat: 5g Total Carbohydrates: 5g Fiber: 1g Sugar: 0g Protein: 11g

DINNER

20. FRENCH COUNTRY CHICKEN

PREPARATION TIME 10 MIN

COOKING TIME 15 MIN

SERVINGS 2

INGREDIENTS:

- 4 boneless chicken breasts
- 1 tbsp. olive oil
- 4 sliced shallots
- 1/4-pound sliced mushrooms
- 1 tbsp. plain flour
- 1 cup low sodium chicken stock
- 1 tbsp. fresh rosemary
- 2 tbsp. chopped parsley
- 1/4 tsp. black pepper
- 1/4 tsp. white pepper
- Salt as per taste

DIRECTIONS:

Place the chicken breasts between wax paper. Flatten the chicken breasts using a mallet.

Cut each chicken breast in half. Cover the chicken breasts with a plastic wrap and refrigerate the breasts till they become firm.

Warm the olive oil in a pan with medium heat. Sauté the shallots in the olive oil for about 3 minutes. Add the mushrooms to the pan and sauté them for about 2 minutes.

Combine 1/4 cup low sodium chicken stock and flour in a bowl.

Add the flour mixture to the pan. Stir in the remaining chicken stock in the pan and cook the mixture over medium heat.

Put salt, black pepper, and white pepper to the sauce. Let the sauce thicken and allow it to cook for 5 minutes. Get the pan from heat and put the rosemary.

Add about a tablespoon of olive oil in a non-stick skillet. Add the chicken breasts till they are no longer pink.

When you want to serve the chicken, breasts transfer them to a platter and add some mushroom sauce over the chicken breasts. Garnish with chopped parsley.

Nutrition: Calories: 210 Total Fat: 8g Total Carbohydrates: 5g Fiber: 0g Sugar: 0g Protein: 27g

21. BEEF STROGANOFF

PREPARATION TIME 10 MIN

COOKING TIME 15 MIN

SERVINGS 2

INGREDIENTS:

- 1/2 cup onion
- 1/2-pound boneless beef (fat removed)
- 4 cups yolkless egg noodles
- 1/2 can fat-free cream of mushroom
- 1 tbsp. all-purpose flour
- 1/2 tsp. paprika
- 1/8 tsp. black pepper
- 1/8 tsp. white pepper
- 1/2 cup fat-free sour cream

DIRECTIONS:

Sauté the onions in a non-stick pan till the onions become translucent.

Add the beef into the pan and continue cooking till the beef turns brown and is tender.

Take the beef from the heat once cooked.

Fill a large pot with water and bring the water to a boil.

Place noodles into the pot and cook as per the packet Directions:.

Drain with cold water once the noodles are cooked.

Add the soup mixture to the non-stick pan. Add the salt, black pepper, white pepper, and paprika to the soup mixture.

Add the beef into this mixture as well, and once the mixture is warmed, remove from heat. Add the sour cream after removing it from heat.

Nutrition: Calories: 391 Total Fat: 23g Total Carbohydrates: 21g Fiber: 1.3g Sugar: 2g Protein: 25g

22. CHIPOTLE SPICED SHRIMP

PREPARATION TIME
5 MIN

COOKING TIME
5 MIN

SERVINGS
2

INGREDIENTS:

- 3/4-pound uncooked shrimp
- 2 tbsp. tomato paste
- 1 1/2 tsp. water
- 1/2 tsp. olive oil
- 1/2 tsp. minced garlic
- 1/2 tsp. chipotle chili powder
- 1/2 tsp. fresh oregano
- 1 tsp. lemon juice
- 1/2 minced green chili

DIRECTIONS:

Clean the shrimp in cold water and pat dry with a paper towel.

Combine oil, water, and tomato paste in a bowl.

Add oregano, chili powder, minced green chili, lemon juice, and garlic to the tomato paste mixture and mix well.

Brush the shrimps with the marinade. Place the shrimps in the refrigerator.

Heat a gas grill. Coat the gas grill with cooking spray. Position the cooking rack four to six inches from the heat source.

Put the shrimp on skewers and put it on the grill. Turn the shrimps after three to four minutes. Transfer the shrimps to a plate once they are cooked.

Nutrition: Calories: 152 Total Fat: 3g Total Carbohydrates: 5g Fiber: 0.3g Sugar: 2g Protein: 24g

23. PIZZA MARGHERITA

PREPARATION TIME 25 MIN

COOKING TIME 10 MIN

SERVINGS 2

INGREDIENTS:

- 2 1/2-inch gluten-free pizza crust
- 1 cup gluten-free pizza sauce
- 2 sliced Roma tomatoes
- 2 sliced capsicum
- 2 tbsp. pesto sauce
- 1 cup low-fat Mozzarella cheese
- 2 tbsp. grated low-fat Parmesan cheese
- 1 tsp. crushed red chili flakes

For Gluten-free Pizza Crust
- 3/4 cup gluten-free flour mix
- 3/4 cup tapioca flour
- 2 tbsp. dry buttermilk powder
- 1 tsp. Agar Agar powder
- 1/2 tsp. salt
- 2 tsp. xanthan gum
- 1 packet dry yeast granule
- 2 tsp. cooking oil
- 1 1/2 tsp. cider vinegar
- 1/2 cup warm water
- Pinch cornmeal

For the pizza sauce
- 1 cup tomato sauce
- 1/2 cup tomato paste
- 1/2 tsp. dried oregano
- 1/2 tsp. dried basil
- 1/2 tsp. onion powder
- 1/4 tsp. garlic powder
- 1 tsp. olive oil
- 1/4 tsp. salt
- 1/2 tsp. black pepper

DIRECTIONS:

Pre-heat your oven to 400 degrees F.

Prepare a baking sheet with parchment paper.

You can sprinkle some cornmeal on the parchment paper.

Put all the dry ingredients in the bowl and mix well.

Add vinegar, cooking oil, and water into the dry ingredients and mix well.

Place the dough on a clean surface and sprinkle it with Tapioca flour. Work the Tapioca flour into the dough in a way that a large ball can be formed. Cut the ball into 2, and this way, you can have 2 pizzas.

Place one pizza crust on the baking sheet. Put some cornmeal on the baking sheet before placing the pizza on it. Bake the pizza crust for 5 minutes first. This helps to make the pizza firm. Repeat this process with the second pizza.

Heat a saucepan over medium heat. Combine all the sauce ingredients in the saucepan and let the sauce simmer for about 10 minutes. This recipe will produce about 12 servings of sauce.

Preheat your oven to 450 degrees F.

To assemble the pizza. Cover both the pizza with the pizza sauce. Add the pesto sauce over both the pizza crusts as well.

Place the sliced tomatoes and Capsicums over both the pizza crusts. Add basil to both the pizzas as well. Next, add the low-fat mozzarella and low-fat Parmesan cheese to the pizzas.

Bake the pizzas on a cooling rack for about 10 minutes till the cheese becomes bubbly and golden. Garnish with red chili flakes in the end.

Nutrition: Calories: 355 Total Fat: 12g Total Carbohydrates: 45g Fiber: 3g Sugar: 4g Protein: 15g

24. CITRUS SALAD

PREPARATION TIME 5 MIN

COOKING TIME 5 MIN

SERVINGS 2

INGREDIENTS:
- 2 oranges
- 1 red grapefruit
- 2 tbsp. orange juice
- 2 tbsp. olive oil
- 1 tsp. lemon juice
- 1 tsp. honey
- 4 cups spring onions
- 2 tbsp. pine nuts
- Pinch salt

DIRECTIONS:

Get the orange and thick slice the top and bottom.

Place the orange in an upright position and remove the thick peel using a sharp knife. Then remove the contour of the fruit.

Get a small bowl and hold the orange then cut along both the sides of each section. Discard the seeds.

Allow the sections and the juice to fall in a bowl. Repeat this process with the second orange and the grapefruit.

Whisk the orange juice, lemon juice, and olive oil in a separate bowl. Put honey and salt to this mixture and mix well.

Divide the green onions into separate plates. Top with the fruits and the dressing mixture. Sprinkle pine nuts on top.

Nutrition: Calories: 100 Total Fat: 0g Total Carbohydrates: 25g Fiber: 1g Sugar: 22g Protein: 1g

25. ROASTED SALMON WITH MAPLE GLAZE

PREPARATION TIME 10 MIN

COOKING TIME 30 MIN

SERVINGS 2

INGREDIENTS:

- 1/4 cup maple syrup
- 1 minced garlic clove
- 1/4 cup balsamic vinegar
- 2 pounds Salmon
- 1/4 tsp. salt
- 1/8 tsp. black pepper
- 1/8 tsp. white pepper
- 1/4 tsp. red chili flakes
- Fresh mint for garnish

DIRECTIONS:

Warm the oven to 450 degrees F. Lightly coat a baking pan with cooking spray.

Place a small saucepan over low heat. Combine maple syrup, balsamic vinegar, and garlic in a small bowl.

Add half of this mixture to a saucepan and heat it till it is a bit hot. Remove the mixture from heat.

Dry the salmon and arrange it on a baking sheet with the skin side facing down. Sprinkle salt, black pepper, white pepper, and red chili flakes on the Salmon.

Brush the fish with maple syrup. Bake it for 10 minutes and brush it again with maple syrup. Bake the fish for another 5 minutes.

Continue basting the fish till it starts to flake.

Transfer to a platter once cooked. Top it with the reserved maple syrup mixture. Garnish with mint.

Nutrition: Calories: 290 Total Fat: 10g Total Carbohydrates: 27g Fiber: 0.1g Sugar: 23g Protein: 23g

26. GARLIC MASHED POTATOES

PREPARATION TIME 5 MIN

COOKING TIME 30 MIN

SERVINGS 2

INGREDIENTS:

- 2 lbs. Potatoes
- 1 tbsp Olive oil
- 2 Garlic cloves
- 4 tbsp Butter
- 1/4 cup Sour cream
- Low-fat cream or milk if needed
- White salt & pepper as per taste

DIRECTIONS:

Separate the garlic into separate cloves.

Pour it into olive oil and wrap it in small pieces of aluminum foil.

Bake in an oven at 350 °F (180 °C) for 30 minutes.

When the garlic cools to the touch, squeeze it from each of the paper shells.

Using a fork, chop the roasted garlic, or use a fine filter to force the chop.

If you use the soup recommended below, crush the garlic and potatoes together.

Peel in brine and boil the potatoes until soft.

Place the chopped potatoes, garlic, sour cream, butter, salt, and white pepper in a blender bowl and stir until smooth at moderate speed.

Add milk or cream for adjusting the consistency.

Nutrition: Calories: 110 Total Fat: 5g Total Carbohydrates: 15g Fiber: 2g Sugar: 2g Protein: 2g

27. TOMATO-BEAN SOUP WITH BREADSTICKS

PREPARATION TIME 10 MIN

COOKING TIME 30 MIN

SERVINGS 2

INGREDIENTS:

- 3 lbs. Ripe tomatoes (fresh)
- 1/2 Diced onion
- 4 cloves Peeled garlic
- 2 tbsp Olive oil
- 1/2 diced Bell pepper (red)
- 1/2 tsp. Basil (dried)
- 2 tbsp. Fresh Herbs parsley/oregano/basil
- Pepper & Salt to taste
- 2 cups Chicken broth
- 1/2 tsp. Dried oregano

DIRECTIONS:

The preheating of the oven at 450 °F is required.

Wash and cut the tomatoes (cut the tomatoes into small pieces and cut them into quarters or one-eighth).

Put tomatoes, garlic, onions, sweet peppers, olive oil, salt, pepper, and dried herbs in a large saucepan.

Set the baking timer to 20 minutes. Stir the saucepan for 5 minutes.

Place the tomatoes for roasting for at least 5 minutes, till some tomatoes have a little charcoaled look.

Bring the chicken broth and add tomatoes and fresh herbs.

Mix the mixture into a smooth and creamy shape using a hand blender.

Serve with fresh basil & parsley.

Nutrition: Calories: 100 Total Fat: 1g Total Carbohydrates: 19g Fiber: 4g Sugar: 3g Protein: 6g

28. BLACKENED CHICKEN WITH BERRY SALAD

PREPARATION TIME
5 MIN

COOKING TIME
15-20 MIN

SERVINGS
2

INGREDIENTS:

- 4 oz. Skinless and boneless chicken breast
- 1 tsp A mixture of Blackening Spice
- 1 cup Romaine lettuce

DIRECTIONS:

Marinate the meat with the mixture of blackening spice and grill at 165°F.

Use the strips of lettuce to make the salad base.

Add radishes, pepper strips, grated carrots, tomato, red cabbage, and peas, as well as pea pods.

Top with your favorite berry mixtures, blueberries, raspberries, and sliced strawberries.

Slice chicken breast into long thin strips and serve them on the salad top.

Add your favorite dressing with low sodium content.

Nutrition: Calories: 251 Total Fat: 14g Total Carbohydrates: 8g Fiber: 2g Sugar: 1.7g Protein: 18g

SNACKS

29. CAJUN POPCORN

PREPARATION TIME
5 MIN

COOKING TIME
5 MIN

SERVINGS
2

INGREDIENTS:

- 4 cups of popped corn
- 1 tbsp butter
- 1/2 tsp smoked paprika
- 1/4 tsp cayenne pepper
- 1/2 tsp ground cumin
- 1/2 tsp garlic powder
- 1/2 tsp onion powder

DIRECTIONS:

In a microwave-safe bowl, combine spices and butter.

Microwave the bowl in 10-second increments and stir until all butter has melted.

Allow the butter to sit for 5 minutes and then reheat until barely warm if needed.

Prepare a large bowl then toss the popcorn and butter mix.

Allow cooling, then divide into snack sized bags of 1 cup each.

Nutrition: Calories: 140 Total Fat: 8g Total Carbohydrates: 15g Fiber: 2g Sugar: 0g Protein: 2g

30. LIME TORTILLA CHIPS

PREPARATION TIME 5 MIN

COOKING TIME 20 MIN

SERVINGS 2

INGREDIENTS:

- 12 corn tortillas (6" cut into 8th triangles)
- 2tbsp oil
- 1tbsp chili powder
- 1 tsp cayenne powder
- 1tsp crushed chipotle pepper
- 1tbsp lime zest
- 1tsp lime juice

DIRECTIONS:

Preheat the oven to 350°F.

Put all the seasonings and the oil in a mixing bowl.

Dip each of the tortilla wedges into the oil mixture and spread them on a non-stick baking sheet.

Bake the chips for 20 minutes until browned and crunchy.

Nutrition: Calories: 150 Total Fat: 7g Total Carbohydrates: 18g Fiber: 1g Sugar: 0.5g Protein: 2g

31. PEACH SALSA

PREPARATION TIME 5 MIN

COOKING TIME 2 MIN

SERVINGS 2

INGREDIENTS:
- 1 Ripe peach diced, and pit removed
- 1 cup chopped mango
- 1 jalapeno pepper seeded and diced
- 2 tbsp lime juice
- 1 ripe/overripe tomato, cored and diced
- 1/2 tsp cinnamon
- 1/2 tsp coriander
- black pepper to taste

DIRECTIONS:
Prepare all the ingredients in the food processor.

Pulse the mixture until smooth, and then pour it into a jar or bowl.

The salsa can be stored 10 days in the fridge.

Nutrition: Calories: 112 Total Fat: 0.7g Total Carbohydrates: 26g Fiber: 4g Sugar: 21g Protein: 3g

32. VEGETABLE CHIPS

PREPARATION TIME
5 MIN

COOKING TIME
30 MIN

SERVINGS
2

INGREDIENTS:

- 2 cups Sliced Sweet Potato
- 2 cups sliced taro root
- 2 cups sliced red beetroot
- 2 cups sliced rutabaga or turnip
- 1/5 cup olive oil
- Seasonings of choice

DIRECTIONS:

Preheat the oven to 275°F.

Mix olive oil and seasonings in a cup.

Pat excess moisture from the vegetables using a paper towel and combine them in a large bowl with the oil mixture.

Spread the coated vegetable slices onto a baking sheet in a single layer.

Bake them 30 minutes, then flip cook until they are crisp.

Remove the vegetables and place them on paper towels to soak excess oils off.

Store the chips for up to 1 week in an airtight container.

Nutrition: Calories: 140 Total Fat: 8g Total Carbohydrates: 16g Fiber: 1g Sugar: 0g Protein: 1g

33. DASH DEVILLED EGGS

PREPARATION TIME 5 MIN

COOKING TIME 10 MIN

SERVINGS 2

INGREDIENTS:

- 12 hard-boiled eggs
- 3 tbsp low-fat mayonnaise
- 1 tbsp mustard
- 1 tbsp onion powder
- 2 tbsp cream cheese or soy cream cheese
- 1 tsp apple cider vinegar
- 1/4 cup sweet relish
- Paprika to Garnish

DIRECTIONS:

Boil eggs for 15 minutes.

Half the eggs and remove yolks into a large bowl. Discard 5-7 of the yolks.

Add mayonnaise, cream cheese, and mustard to egg yolks and combine until smooth.

Add vinegar, relish, and onion powder, then stir the mixture vigorously.

Arrange the yolk mixture into a piping bag or clear plastic sandwich bag.

Pipe it into the empty egg halves. Chill the eggs until ready to serve.

Nutrition: Calories: 55 Total Fat: 4g Total Carbohydrates: 0.4g Fiber: 0g Sugar: 0.3g Protein: 3g

34. VANILLA LEMON PARFAIT

PREPARATION TIME
5 MIN

COOKING TIME
10 MIN

SERVINGS
2

INGREDIENTS:

- 1 cup Greek yogurt
- 1/4 tsp vanilla extract
- 1 tsp honey
- Zest of 1 lemon plus 1/4 tsp juice
- 1/4 cup chopped pistachios
- 1/4 cup whole grain granola or dry oatmeal

DIRECTIONS:

In a small bowl, combine yogurt, vanilla, lemon, and honey.

Stir the yogurt until smooth and set aside.

In a tall glass, arrange the granola, yogurt, and pistachios.

Drizzle the top with more honey and granola if desired.

Nutrition: Calories: 140 Total Fat: 6g Total Carbohydrates: 22g Fiber: 1g Sugar: 13g Protein: 11g

35. FIGS WITH GOAT CHEESE

PREPARATION TIME
5 MIN

COOKING TIME
6 MIN

SERVINGS
2

INGREDIENTS:

- 4 large fresh figs washed and halved
- 4oz crumbled goat cheese
- 4 tbsp honey
- 1/4cup pecans

DIRECTIONS:

Preheat the oven to 350°F.

On a medium baking sheet, arrange figs with skin side down.

Spoon the goat's cheese on top of each fig half and top them with pecans.

Bake for 6 minutes until cheese has softened but not browned.

Remove from heat and drizzle them gently with honey.

Figs can be eaten hot or cold, but they do taste amazing when straight from the oven.

Nutrition: Calories: 90 Total Fat: 7g Total Carbohydrates: 3g Fiber: 0g Sugar: 3g Protein: 3g

CHAPTER 3. 2 WEEKS METABOLISM-BOOSTING MENU

DAY	BREAKFAST	LUNCH	DINNER	SNACK
1	BLUEBERRY OAT PANCAKES	BROCCOLI, GARLIC, AND RIGATONI	AVOCADO CUCUMBER SOUP	PINEAPPLE SUNDAE
2	PERFECT GRANOLA	PASTA WITH SPINACH, GARBANZOS, AND RAISINS	GREEK FETA SALAD	ICED ESPRESSO LATTE
3	FRUIT AND GRAIN BREAKFAST	STUFFED EGGPLANT	RUSSIAN COLD SOUP	PEACH PARFAIT
4	GREEN BREAKFAST SMOOTHIE	STEAK TACOS	FRUITY LAMB'S LETTUCE	MINTY-LIME ICED TEA
5	MUSHROOM AND SHALLOT FRITTATA	ACORN SQUASH WITH APPLES	OLIVE PESTO	BERRY SMOOTHIE
6	CHEESE AND BROCCOLI MINI EGG OMELETS	BROILED WHITE SEA BASS	ORANGE N CHICORY SALAD	PBA SANDWICH
7	BANANA-NUT PANCAKES	MANGO SALSA PIZZA	WHOLE GRAIN BRUSCHETTA	FRUIT SMOOTHIES
8	NO-BAKE BREAKFAST GRANOLA BARS	CHICKEN ALFREDO WITH WHOLE-WHEAT BOWTIE PASTA	MACKEREL TAPAS	PEACH PARFAIT

9	BANANA AND PEANUT BUTTER BREAKFAST SMOOTHIE	BROCCOLI, GARLIC, AND RIGATONI	BELL PEPPER MACKEREL	MINTY-LIME ICED TEA
10	APPLE-SPICE BAKED OATMEAL	SPINACH MUSHROOM FRITTATA	AVOCADO CUCUMBER SOUP	PBA SANDWICH
11	GREEN BREAKFAST SMOOTHIE	BROILED WHITE SEA BASS	FRUITY LAMB'S LETTUCE	ICED ESPRESSO LATTE
12	FRUIT AND GRAIN BREAKFAST	ACORN SQUASH WITH APPLES	GREEK FETA SALAD	PINEAPPLE SUNDAE
13	PERFECT GRANOLA	BROILED WHITE SEA BASS	RUSSIAN COLD SOUP	BERRY SMOOTHIE
14	BLUEBERRY OAT PANCAKES	STEAK TACOS	OLIVE PESTO	

BREAKFAST

36. NO-BAKE BREAKFAST GRANOLA BARS

PREPARATION TIME 10 MIN

COOKING TIME 30 MIN

SERVINGS 28

INGREDIENTS:

- 2 1/2 cup toasted rice cereal
- 2 cups old-fashioned oatmeal
- 1/2 cup raisins
- 1/2 cup brown sugar firmly packed
- 1/2 cup light corn syrup
- 1/2 cup peanut butter
- 1 tsp. vanilla

DIRECTIONS:

Prepare rice, cereal, raisins, in a bowl and stir together well with a spoon.

Put the brown sugar and syrup in a saucepan. Stir the mixture continuously while bringing it to a boil, and then remove from heat.

Put peanut butter and vanilla. Mix until well-blended.

Add peanut butter mixture over the cereal and raisins in the mixing bowl and combine well.

Press the mixture into a 13 x 9-inch baking pan and cut into 18 bars.

Refrigerate for 30 minutes.

Nutrition: Calories: 207 Total Fat: 5g Total Carbohydrates: 38g Fiber: 3g Sugar: 20g Protein: 4g

37. BANANA AND PEANUT BUTTER BREAKFAST SMOOTHIE

PREPARATION TIME
5 MIN

COOKING TIME
5 MIN

SERVINGS
2

INGREDIENTS:

- 1 c. non-fat milk
- 1 T. all-natural peanut butter
- 1 medium banana

DIRECTIONS:

Prepare all ingredients in a blender and mix until smooth.

Serve and enjoy!

Nutrition: Calories: 230 Total Fat: 9g Total Carbohydrates: 30g Fiber: 2g Sugar: 4g Protein: 10g

38. APPLE-SPICE BAKED OATMEAL

PREPARATION TIME 10 MIN

COOKING TIME 30 MIN

SERVINGS 2

INGREDIENTS:

- 1 egg, beaten
- 1/2 c. sweetened applesauce
- 1/2 c. non-fat or 1% milk
- 1 tsp. vanilla
- 2 T. oil
- 1 apple, chopped
- 2 c. rolled oats
- 1 tsp. Baking powder
- 1/4 tsp. salt
- 1 tsp. cinnamon
- 2 T. brown sugar
- 2 T. chopped nuts

DIRECTIONS:

Prepare and warm the oven to 375° F. Lightly oil an 8 x 8-inch baking pan.

Mix applesauce, egg, milk, vanilla, and oil in a bowl, then add in the apple.

In another bowl, combine baking powder, rolled oats, cinnamon, and salt, and add this to the liquid mixture. Mix well.

Get the mixture and pour into the prepared baking dish. Bake for about 25 minutes.

Remove from the oven when done and sprinkle with brown sugar and nuts. Allow broiling in the oven for an additional 3-4 minutes until the top is brown and sugar bubbles start to appear.

Cut into squares and serve warm.

Nutrition: Calories: 160 Total Fat: 6g Total Carbohydrates: 22g Fiber: 3g Sugar: 0g Protein: 6g

PREPARATION TIME
10 MIN

COOKING TIME
20 MIN

SERVINGS
2

39. BANANA-NUT PANCAKES

INGREDIENTS:
- 1 c. whole-wheat flour
- 2 tsp. Baking powder
- 1/4 tsp. Salt
- 1/4 tsp. cinnamon
- 1 large banana, mashed
- 1 c. 1% milk
- 3 large egg whites
- 2 tsp. oil
- 1 tsp. vanilla
- 2 T. walnuts, chopped

DIRECTIONS:
Put and mix well all dry ingredients in a large bowl.

In a different bowl, mix oil, milk, egg whites, mashed bananas, and vanilla until smooth.

Add now the wet ingredients with the dry, but DO NOT over mix.

Heat a large skillet over medium heat and lightly spray with cooking oil. Pour around 1/4 cup of the pancake batter on the hot skillet.

When the batter starts to set and bubble, flip it over. Repeat with the remaining batter.

Nutrition: Calories: 114 Total Fat: 5g Total Carbohydrates: 16g Fiber: 0g Sugar: 0g Protein: 20g

40. CHEESE AND BROCCOLI MINI EGG OMELETS

PREPARATION TIME 10 MIN

COOKING TIME 30 MIN

SERVINGS 2

INGREDIENTS:

- 2 c. broccoli florets
- 4 eggs
- 1 c. egg whites
- 1/4c. reduced-fat cheddar cheese
- 1/4c. grated Romano or parmesan cheese
- 1 tbsp. olive oil
- Salt and pepper to taste
- Cooking spray

DIRECTIONS:

Preheat oven to 350° F.

In a small saucepan, steam broccoli with water for about 6-7 minutes.

Once broccoli is cooked, drain well, then mash with salt, pepper, and oil.

Spray some cooking oil to a muffin tin, then spoon broccoli evenly into each muffin well.

In a separate bowl, beat egg whites, grated parmesan cheese, eggs, salt, and pepper.

Pour this mixture into the spooned broccoli mixture in the muffin pan.

Put some grated cheddar on top and bake for 20 minutes. Serve immediately.

Nutrition: Calories: 167 Total Fat: 8g Total Carbohydrates: 5g Fiber: 2g Sugar: 0g Protein: 18g

41. MUSHROOM AND SHALLOT FRITTATA

PREPARATION TIME: 10 MIN
COOKING TIME: 30 MIN
SERVINGS: 2

INGREDIENTS:

- 1 T. unsalted butter
- 4 shallots, finely chopped
- 1/2 lb. mushrooms
- 2 T. fresh parsley, finely chopped
- 1 tsp. dried thyme
- 3 eggs
- black pepper to taste
- 5 large egg whites
- 1 T. milk or fat-free half-and-half
- 1/4c. fresh-grated parmesan cheese

DIRECTIONS:

Preheat oven to 350° F.

Warm and melt butter in a large, oven-safe skillet. Stir in shallots and sauté until golden brown.

Add parsley, thyme, mushrooms, and black pepper.

Get another bowl then whisk eggs and egg whites together with parmesan cheese and milk.

Add the egg mixture to the skillet.

When the edges begin to set, place the entire skillet in the oven.

Bake until frittata is fully cooked, about 15 minutes.

Cut into four wedges and serve.

Nutrition: Calories: 132 Total Fat: 7g Total Carbohydrates: 6g Fiber: 0g Sugar: 0g Protein: 10g

42. GREEN BREAKFAST SMOOTHIE

PREPARATION TIME
5 MIN

COOKING TIME
5 MIN

SERVINGS
2

INGREDIENTS:

- 1 medium banana
- 1 c. baby spinach
- 1/2 c. fat-free milk
- 1/4 c. whole oats
- 3/4 c. frozen mango
- 1/4 c. plain non-fat yogurt
- 1/2 tsp. vanilla

DIRECTIONS:

Prepare blender and put all ingredients. Mix well.

Serve immediately.

Nutrition: Calories: 265 Total Fat: 13g Total Carbohydrates: 25g Fiber: 0g Sugar: 0g Protein: 13g

PREPARATION TIME
10 MIN

COOKING TIME
15 MIN

SERVINGS
2

43. FRUIT AND GRAIN BREAKFAST

INGREDIENTS:

- 3 c. water
- 1/4 tsp. salt
- 3/4 c. quick-cooking brown rice
- 3/4 c. bulgur
- 1 granny Smith apple
- 1 red apple
- 1 orange
- 1 c. raisins
- 1 (8 oz.) c. low-fat vanilla yogurt

DIRECTIONS:

Heat water and salt in a large pot over high heat.

Reduce heat to low after adding rice and bulgur, then cover and cook for 10 minutes.

Take it from the heat and let stand for 2 minutes.

Spread the hot grains to cool on a baking sheet.

Prepare the fruit, then transfer the chilled grains and cut fruit into a mixing bowl.

Add in the yogurt. Serve.

Nutrition: Calories: 140 Total Fat: 2g Total Carbohydrates: 27g Fiber: 2g Sugar: 12g Protein: 2g

44. PERFECT GRANOLA

PREPARATION TIME 10 MIN

COOKING TIME 30 MIN

SERVINGS 24

INGREDIENTS:
- 1/4 c. canola oil
- 4 T. honey
- 1 1/2 tsp. vanilla
- 6 c. rolled oats
- 1 c. slivered almonds
- 1/2 c. unsweetened cocoa
- 2 c. bran flakes
- 3/4 c. walnuts
- 1 c. raisins

DIRECTIONS:

Preheat oven to 350° F.

Put oil, honey, and vanilla to a saucepan then cook over low heat.

Add all remaining ingredients to a large mixing bowl and mix well.

Stir in the honey-oil mixture, making sure the grains are all evenly coated.

Prepare a lightly greased baking pan then spread the cereal mixture. Bake in the oven for 25 minutes until slightly brown.

Add the raisins and spread throughout the mixture.

Nutrition: Calories: 110 Total Fat: 1g Total Carbohydrates: 21g Fiber: 2g Sugar: 5g Protein: 3g

45. BLUEBERRY OAT PANCAKES

PREPARATION TIME 10 MIN

COOKING TIME 20 MIN

SERVINGS 2

INGREDIENTS:

- 1 1/2 c. water
- 1/2 c. steel-cut oats
- 1/8 tsp. salt
- 1 c. whole-wheat flour
- 1/2 tsp. Baking powder
- 1/2 tsp. baking soda
- 1 egg
- 1 c. milk
- 1/2 c. Greek yogurt
- 1 c. frozen blueberries
- 1/2 c. + 2 T. agave nectar

DIRECTIONS:

Put some water to a pot and bring to a boil. Add the oats. Stir to combine and cook until tender.

In a mixing bowl, combine the whole-wheat pastry flour, baking powder, baking soda, milk, egg, and yogurt until a batter is formed.

Gently fold in the blueberries and rolled oats.

On a non-stick skillet, pour about 1/4c. of batter and cook each pancake until golden.

Serve stacked pancakes with a garnish of agave nectar.

Nutrition: Calories: 195 Total Fat: 1g Total Carbohydrates: 25g Fiber: 5g Sugar: 8g Protein: 22g

LUNCH

46. STEAK TACOS

PREPARATION TIME
10 MIN

COOKING TIME
15-20 MIN

SERVINGS
2

INGREDIENTS:

- 1/4 pounds sirloin steak
- 1/4 teaspoon salt
- Freshly ground black pepper, to taste
- 2 tablespoons plus 2 teaspoons olive oil
- 12 (6-inch) tortillas
- 1/2 red onion, diced
- Fresh jalapeno peppers, seeded and chopped
- 1/2 bunch fresh cilantro, chopped
- limes, cut into wedges

DIRECTIONS:

Cut the steak into strips.

Warm 2 tbsp. olive oil on medium-high heat.

Put in steak and sauté until browned on all sides and cooked through to the desired doneness, about 5-6 minutes.

Sprinkle with salt and pepper. Put in the pan on a plate and cover to keep warm.

In the same skillet, pour in 2 more teaspoons olive oil and let it get hot.

Put in tortillas, one at a time, and cook, turning once, until the tortilla is lightly browned but still flexible.

To arrange tacos, lay the tortilla on a plate, and place steak, onion, jalapeno peppers, and cilantro on top of it. Squeeze lime juice over the top.

Nutrition: Calories: 289 Total Fat: 15g Total Carbohydrates: 15g Fiber: 4g Sugar: 1g Protein: 24g

47. PASTA WITH SPINACH, GARBANZOS, AND RAISINS

PREPARATION TIME 10 MIN

COOKING TIME 15 MIN

SERVINGS 2

INGREDIENTS:

- 8 ounces farfalle (bowtie) pasta
- 2 tablespoons olive oil
- 4 garlic cloves, crushed
- 1/2 can (19 ounces) garbanzos, rinsed and drained
- 1/2 cup unsalted chicken broth
- 1/2 cup golden raisins
- 4 cups fresh spinach, chopped
- 2 tablespoons Parmesan cheese
- Cracked black peppercorns, to taste

DIRECTIONS:

Fill about 75% of a large pot with water and bring to a boil.

Put in the pasta and cook until tender 10 to 12 minutes, or according to the package Directions:. Drain the pasta completely.

Warm olive oil and garlic on a skillet with medium heat.

Put in the garbanzos and chicken broth. Stir until warmed through.

Put raisins and spinach. Cook spinach about 3 minutes. Do not overcook.

Divide the pasta on plates. Put 1/6 of the sauce, 1 teaspoon Parmesan cheese, and peppercorns on top of each serving to taste. Serve instantly.

Nutrition: Calories: 283 Total Fat: 7g Total Carbohydrates: 44g Fiber: 7g Sugar: 12g Protein: 11g

48. MANGO SALSA PIZZA

PREPARATION TIME 10 MIN

COOKING TIME 15 MIN

SERVINGS 2

INGREDIENTS:

- 12-inch prepared whole-grain pizza crust, purchased or made from a mix
- 1/2 cup onion
- 1/2 cup mango
- 1 cup red or green bell peppers
- 1/2 cup pineapple (tidbits)
- 1 tbsp. lime juice
- 1/2 cup fresh cilantro

DIRECTIONS:

Prepare the oven to 425 F. Slightly covers a 12-inch round baking pan with cooking spray.

Chopped onion, bell peppers and cilantro.

Prepare the mango, chopped, seeded and peeled.

Put peppers, onions, mango, pineapple, lime juice, and cilantro in a small bowl. Set aside.

Get and roll out dough. Press into the baking pan. Keep in the oven and cook for about 15 minutes.

Get the pizza crust out of the oven and cover it with mango salsa. Put it back into the oven. Bake for 5 minutes or more until the toppings are hot and the crust is browned.

Slice the pizza into 8 even slices and serve instantly.

Nutrition: Calories: 249 Total Fat: 5g Total Carbohydrates: 49g Fiber: 8g Sugar: 0g Protein: 8g

PREPARATION TIME
15 MIN

COOKING TIME
30 MIN

SERVINGS
2

49. STUFFED EGGPLANT

INGREDIENTS:

- medium eggplant
- 1 cup of water
- 1 tbsp. olive oil
- 6 ounces boneless, skinless chicken breast
- 1/4 cup onion, chopped
- 1/4 cup red, green, or yellow bell peppers chopped
- 1/4 cup celery chopped
- 1/2 cup sliced fresh mushrooms
- 1 cup whole-wheat breadcrumbs
- Freshly ground black pepper, to taste
- 1 cup unsalted tomatoes (canned), drained except for 1/4 cup liquid

DIRECTIONS:

Preheat the oven to 350 F. Slightly covers a baking dish with cooking spray.

Cut chicken breast into strips 1/2-inch-wide and 2 inches long.

Trim the ends off the eggplant and chop in half lengthwise. Using a spoon, remove pulp, leaving a thick shell.

Prepare the baking dish and lay out the shells then pour water into the bottom of the dish. Cut the eggplant pulp into cubes. Set aside.

Put oil in a large nonstick frying pan, heat over medium-high.

Put in the chicken strips and sauté until the chicken is slightly browned and no longer pink, about 5 minutes.

Put diced eggplant, onion, peppers, tomatoes, and reserved tomato juice, celery, and mushrooms to the chicken.

Let it simmer with lower heat until the vegetables are tender about 10 minutes.

Put black pepper and breadcrumbs. Add half mixture into each eggplant shell.

Enfold with aluminum foil. Bake for 15 minutes or more until the eggplant softened and stuffing is cooked through.

Move eggplant to individual plates and serve instantly.

Nutrition: Calories: 310 Total Fat: 9g Total Carbohydrates: 33g Fiber: 6g Sugar: 5g Protein: 27g

50. ACORN SQUASH WITH APPLES

PREPARATION TIME
5 MIN

COOKING TIME
10 MIN

SERVINGS
2

INGREDIENTS:

- Granny Smith apple
- 1 small acorn squash
- tbsp. brown sugar
- teaspoons trans-free margarine

DIRECTIONS:

Peeled, cored, and sliced the apple.

Prepare apple and brown sugar in a bowl. Set aside.

Prick the squash several times with a sharp knife to let the steam out during cooking.

Place in the microwave with high temperature until tender, about 5 minutes. Flip the squash after 3 minutes to make sure it cooks evenly.

Slice the squash in half. Remove the seeds out of the center of each half.

Put the apple mixture in the squash.

Place the squash back into the microwave and cook until the apples are softened about 2 minutes.

Serve with 1 teaspoon of margarine on each top.

Nutrition: Calories: 204 Total Fat: 4g Total Carbohydrates: 40g Fiber: 6g Sugar: 6g Protein: 2g

PREPARATION TIME
5 MIN

COOKING TIME
10 MIN

SERVINGS
2

51. BROILED WHITE SEA BASS

INGREDIENTS:
- 2 white sea bass fillets (4 ounces)
- 1 tablespoon lemon juice
- 1 teaspoon garlic, minced
- 1/4 teaspoon salt-free herbed seasoning blend
- Ground black pepper, to taste

DIRECTIONS:

Preheat the broiler or grill.

Slightly coat a baking pan with cooking spray. Lay the fillets in the pan.

Drizzle the lemon juice, garlic, herbed seasoning, and pepper over the fillets.

Broil (grill) until the fish is opaque all over when tested with a tip of a knife, about 8 to 10 minutes. Serve instantly.

Nutrition: Calories: 114 Total Fat: 2g Total Carbohydrates: 2g Fiber: 1g Sugar: 0g Protein: 21g

52. CHICKEN ALFREDO WITH WHOLE-WHEAT BOWTIE PASTA

PREPARATION TIME
10 MIN

COOKING TIME
30 MIN

SERVINGS
2

INGREDIENTS:

- 12 ounces whole-wheat bowtie pasta
- 2 tablespoons olive oil
- 3 chicken breasts, boneless and skinless
- 2 cloves garlic
- 3/4 low-sodium chicken broth
- 1/2 cup half-and-half
- 3/4 cup grated Parmesan cheese
- 2 tablespoons fresh parsley, minced
- Freshly ground black pepper, to taste

DIRECTIONS:

Cook pasta per the package instructions. Set aside.

Put 2 tablespoons of olive oil on a skillet with medium-high heat.

Put in chicken breasts and cook until golden brown and done in the middle, about 5-6 minutes per side. Take out of the pan, chop into bite-size pieces, set aside.

Pour in the remaining 2 tablespoons of olive oil into the pan. Put garlic and sauté for a minute.

Add broth and let it boil for about 2 minutes. Put in half-and-half and whisk together. Carry on cooking, stirring regularly, for several minutes until liquid begins to become thick.

Turn off the heat and put in Parmesan cheese, chicken, and pasta. Sprinkle with black pepper.

Toss all ingredients together until well mixed.

Serve with parsley and additional parmesan cheese on top, if desired.

Nutrition: Calories: 295 Total Fat: 10g Total Carbohydrates: 33g Fiber: 6g Sugar: 3g Protein: 17g

53. BROCCOLI, GARLIC, AND RIGATONI

PREPARATION TIME 10 MIN

COOKING TIME 25 MIN

SERVINGS 2

INGREDIENTS:

- 1/3-pound rigatoni noodles
- 2 cups broccoli florets (tops)
- 2 tablespoons Parmesan cheese
- 2 teaspoons olive oil
- 2 teaspoons minced garlic
- Freshly ground black pepper, to taste

DIRECTIONS:

Fill about 75% of a large pot with water and bring to a boil. Put in the pasta and cook until tender, 10 to 12 minutes, or according to the package Directions:. Drain the pasta completely.

As the pasta cooks, in a pot fitted with a steamer basket, bring 1 inch of water to a boil. Put in the broccoli, cover, and steam until tender, about 10 minutes.

Get a large bowl then mix the cooked pasta and broccoli. Toss with Parmesan cheese, olive oil, and garlic.

Sprinkle with pepper to taste. Serve instantly.

Nutrition: Calories: 340 Total Fat: 8g Total Carbohydrates: 50g Fiber: 8g Sugar: 3g Protein: 16g

54. SPINACH MUSHROOM FRITTATA

PREPARATION TIME 10 MIN

COOKING TIME 15 MIN

SERVINGS 2

INGREDIENTS:

- 3 cloves of garlic, minced
- 1 cup chopped onion
- 1 teaspoon olive oil
- 1/2-pound fresh mushrooms, sliced
- 1/2 teaspoon dried thyme
- 10-ounce-bag fresh spinach
- 1 tbsp. water
- 1 tsp. dried dill or 1 tbsp. fresh dill
- Egg substitute equivalent to 10 eggs
- 1/4 teaspoon black pepper
- 1/4 cup feta cheese

DIRECTIONS:

Prepare oven to 350 degrees F.

In a 10- or 12-inch nonstick, ovenproof skillet, sauté garlic and onion in olive oil for around 5 minutes.

Put in mushrooms and thyme. Cook for 5 minutes more. Take the skillet off the stove.

Put spinach in a separate saucepan. Pour in 1 tablespoon of water. Cover and cook until just wilted. Drain spinach and let cool in a strainer. Squeeze out any liquid. Slice leaves.

In a large bowl, beat together egg substitute, dill, and pepper. Mix in the spinach, mushroom mixture, and feta cheese.

Clean nonstick skillet. Coat well with cooking spray. Put skillet back on the stove over medium heat. When the skillet is hot, add egg mixture.

Place in oven, uncovered. Check frittata in 10 minutes. Do not overcook.

When done, place a large serving platter over the skillet. Flip skillet over so that frittata falls onto the plate. Chop into six pieces and serve.

Nutrition: Calories: 123 Total Fat: 4g Total Carbohydrates: 4g Fiber: 0g Sugar: 1g Protein: 15g

DINNER

55. AVOCADO CUCUMBER SOUP

PREPARATION TIME
10 MIN

COOKING TIME
20-30 MIN

SERVINGS
2

INGREDIENTS:

- 1/2 cucumber
- 1 small spring onion
- 1 avocado pulp
- Juice of 1/2 lime
- 1 tbsp chives (chopped up)
- Fresh black pepper
- 1 low-fat yogurt
- 1 slice of whole-grain bread

DIRECTIONS:

Prepare the cucumber by peeling and cut it into pieces.

Remove the pulp from the avocado.

Wash and chop the spring onions.

Put everything together with the yogurt and the juice of the 1/2 lime in a blender and puree.

Then place in a soup plate, garnish with the chives, and pour some fresh black pepper over it.

Enjoy with the slice of whole meal bread.

Nutrition: Calories: 169 Total Fat: 8g Total Carbohydrates: 15g Fiber: 3g Sugar: 8g Protein: 12g

56. WHOLE GRAIN BRUSCHETTA

PREPARATION TIME 10 MIN

COOKING TIME 20 MIN

SERVINGS 2

INGREDIENTS:

- 4 slices of whole-grain baguette (approx. 2 cm thick)
- 2 medium-sized tasty tomatoes
- 5 small mozzarella balls
- 1 teaspoon parsley (chopped)
- 6 basil leaves
- 1 clove of garlic (chopped) (alternatively: wild garlic leaves)
- 1/2 fennel (cut into cubes)
- 1 tsp - 1 tbsp olive oil
- 1 dash of balsamic vinegar
- 1 pinch of black pepper (fresh)

DIRECTIONS:

Rinse tomatoes and cut them into small cubes. If you prefer a dry topping, remove the seeds from the tomatoes beforehand (with your finger or a teaspoon)

Wash the fennel and cut into small cubes.

Chop the herbs and the clove of garlic.

Put all ingredients in a bowl, season with olive oil, balsamic vinegar, and pepper. Stir well.

Cut the whole grain baguette in approx. Cut 2 cm slices and toast.

Halve the mozzarella balls and arrange them on the toast with the tomatoes.

Nutrition: Calories: 206 Total Fat: 4g Total Carbohydrates: 35g Fiber: 2g Sugar: 0.2g Protein: 7g

57. RUSSIAN COLD SOUP

PREPARATION TIME 10 MIN

COOKING TIME 30 MIN

SERVINGS 2

INGREDIENTS:

- 1/4 cucumber
- 1 spring onion
- 1/2 bunch of dill
- 3 radishes
- 150 g natural yogurt (lean)
- 1 egg (hard-boiled)
- 2 small jacket potatoes
- 50g lean cooked ham
- some mineral water
- a little vinegar

DIRECTIONS:

First, hard- boil the egg and cook the jacket potatoes through.

In the meantime, cut the spring onion and dill very small and place in a bowl.

Dice the cooked ham and add to it.

Wash radishes and cucumber cut into very small cubes and add.

Add the natural yogurt and stir everything together.

As soon as the potatoes and egg are ready, cut both into small cubes and add them.

Add a little mineral water so that it has the consistency of a soup.

Season with a little vinegar.

Nutrition: Calories: 55 Total Fat: 2g Total Carbohydrates: 4g Fiber: 0g Sugar: 0g Protein: 3g

58. GREEK FETA SALAD

PREPARATION TIME
10 MIN

COOKING TIME
10 MIN

SERVINGS
2

INGREDIENTS:

- 1 tomato
- 1 bell pepper
- 60 g feta
- 1 handful of leaves from lettuce
- 1/4 cucumber
- 20 g walnut kernels
- 1 tbsp olive oil
- Juice of 1 lemon
- 1 tbsp wild garlic (cut into small pieces)
- 1 teaspoon parsley (cut into small pieces)
- 1 teaspoon chives (cut into small pieces)
- Pinch of black pepper (fresh)

DIRECTIONS:

Wash the cucumber well or peel and dice.

Wash the bell peppers, remove the seeds and inner skins and cut into thin strips.

Wash tomatoes, remove seeds, and cut into wedges.

Cut the feta into cubes.

Chop the herbs.

Chop the walnuts.

Put the ingredients in a bowl and season with olive oil, lemon juice, and pepper.

Nutrition: Calories: 150 Total Fat: 13g Total Carbohydrates: 6g Fiber: 3g Sugar: 0g Protein: 2g

59. OLIVE PESTO

PREPARATION TIME 10 MIN

COOKING TIME 10 MIN

SERVINGS 2

INGREDIENTS:
- 10 black olives
- 1 clove of garlic (alternatively: 1 tbsp wild garlic leaves)
- 1 tbsp basil (fresh)
- 1 tbsp olive oil
- 2 teaspoons parmesan
- 20 g pine nuts
- 1 whole-grain pita roll
- 1 medium-sized tasty tomato.

DIRECTIONS:
Core the olives and puree them together with the herbs, parmesan, olive oil, and garlic clove, or put them in a blender.

Wash and slice tomatoes.

Warm pita bread on the toaster. Then brush the inside with pesto and add a few pine nuts and tomato slices.

Nutrition: Calories: 230 Total Fat: 23g Total Carbohydrates: 4g Fiber: 2g Sugar: 1g Protein: 2g

PREPARATION TIME
10 MIN

COOKING TIME
15 MIN

SERVINGS
2

60. MACKEREL TAPAS

INGREDIENTS:

- 200 g mackerel (preferably fresh; otherwise 60 g mackerel fillets)
- 1 red pepper
- 1 small onion
- 6 black olives
- 1 tbsp parsley (chopped)
- 1 tbsp olive oil
- 1 teaspoon lemon juice
- 1 pinch of black pepper
- Coconut fat
- Ras-el-Hanout (or paprika)
- 4 slices of whole-grain baguette

DIRECTIONS:

Put mackerel in a pan with a little coconut oil and fry briefly.

Season with Ras-el-Hanout or paprika. Put cover and wait for it to simmer for about 10 minutes until it is well done.

Wash the peppers and herbs, cut into small pieces, and place in a bowl.

Peel and chop the onion and add.

Season to taste with olive oil, lemon juice, and pepper.

Cut the mackerel into cubes.

Toast the wholegrain baguette and top with the mackerel cubes and vegetables.

Nutrition: Calories: 230 Total Fat: 9g Total Carbohydrates: 0g Fiber: 0g Sugar: 0g Protein: 34g

61. ORANGE N CHICORY SALAD

PREPARATION TIME 10 MIN

COOKING TIME 10 MIN

SERVINGS 2

INGREDIENTS:

- 2 medium-sized chicory
- 1 orange
- 1/2 red onion
- 100 g low-fat yogurt
- 1 teaspoon olive oil (or grapeseed oil)
- black pepper
- 1 pinch of curry
- 1 splash of agave syrup (optional, if you like it sweeter)

DIRECTIONS:

Wash the chicory, remove the bitter stalk, and cut into fine strips.

Halve the orange, peel, cut into cubes, and place in a bowl with the chicory.

Chop the onion and add it.

Squeeze the rest of the orange and mix with the yogurt and olive oil. Season with pepper and curry, pour over the chicory, and mix.

Nutrition: Calories: 143 Total Fat: 12g Total Carbohydrates: 8g Fiber: 0g Sugar: 0g Protein: 2g

PREPARATION TIME
10 MIN

COOKING TIME
10 MIN

SERVINGS
2

62. FRUITY LAMB'S LETTUCE

INGREDIENTS:

- 1 handful of lamb's lettuces
- 100 g strawberries
- 20 g walnut kernels (crushed)
- 2 radishes
- 1 tbsp olive oil
- 1 tbsp watercress
- 1 tsp balsamic vinegar
- 2 drops of honey
- 1 pinch of fresh black pepper

DIRECTIONS:

Sort out the lamb's lettuce, clean it, wash it thoroughly, and let it drain well.

Wash the radishes, cut them into small sticks.

Wash the strawberries.

The walnut kernels mince.

Wash the cress, pat dry, and cut finely.

For the dressing, mix olive oil, vinegar, honey, pepper, and cress.

Arrange the salad in a bowl and carefully pour the dressing over the salad, and fold in.

Nutrition: Calories: 200 Total Fat: 9g Total Carbohydrates: 34g Fiber: 9g Sugar: 6g Protein: 8g

63. BELL PEPPER MACKEREL

PREPARATION TIME 10 MIN

COOKING TIME 15-20 MIN

SERVINGS 2

INGREDIENTS:

- 450 g mackerel (preferably fresh; otherwise 100 g mackerel fillets)
- 2 pointed peppers (alternatively: 1/2 yellow, 1/2 red peppers)
- 1 tomato
- 1 small onion
- Coconut fat
- 1 teaspoon thyme leaves
- 1 tbsp wild garlic (cut)
- 4 black olives
- black pepper (fresh)
- 4 slices of whole-grain baguette

DIRECTIONS:

Clean, core, and cut the bell pepper into strips.

Wash tomato and cut into slices.

Peel the onion and cut it into rings.

Prepare the herbs.

Sauté onions in a pan with a little coconut fat until they are translucent.

Wash the mackerel, dry it, put it in the pan and fry it briefly.

Then add the bell pepper and tomato slices and pour the herbs on top.

Put a lid on the pan and cook for about 10-12 minutes.

Cut the olives into slices and lightly toast the whole grain baguette.

Arrange the fish on a plate. Garnish with olive slices and sprinkle with a little black pepper.

Nutrition: Calories: 270 Total Fat: 21g Total Carbohydrates: 4g Fiber: 2g Sugar: 0g Protein: 22g

SNACK

64. PINEAPPLE SUNDAE

PREPARATION TIME 5 MIN

COOKING TIME 30 MIN

SERVINGS 2

INGREDIENTS:

- Container Pineapple (Juice Pack)
- 1 tablespoon Vanilla Yogurt
- 2 tablespoons artificial sweeteners
- 1 tablespoon chopped Dry Roasted Sunflower Kernels or Dry Roasted Pistachio Nuts

DIRECTIONS:

Add vanilla yogurt to a glass and top it with pineapple tidbits.

Sprinkle sunflower kernels or pistachio nuts.

Chill and enjoy!

Nutrition: Calories: 230 Total Fat: 7g Total Carbohydrates: 37g Fiber: 0g Sugar: 32g Protein: 5.6g

PREPARATION TIME
5 MIN

COOKING TIME
5 MIN

SERVINGS
2

65. PEACH PARFAIT

INGREDIENTS:

- 1 cup, sliced and fresh Peaches
- 1 1/2 cup, low-fat or fat-free Milk
- 1/8 tablespoon extract Almond
- 1 cup fresh Raspberry

DIRECTIONS:

Add milk, peaches, and almond extract to the blender and allow it to smoothen up.

Take a fork and mash the raspberries.

Take a glass and pour the 2 mixtures, raspberries and milk in the glass.

Nutrition: Calories: 120 Total Fat: 2g Total Carbohydrates: 24g Fiber: 0g Sugar: 0g Protein: 0g

66. PBA SANDWICH

PREPARATION TIME 5 MIN

COOKING TIME 10 MIN

SERVINGS 2

INGREDIENTS:
- 1 sliced Apple
- 1 tablespoon Honey
- 1 tablespoon Peanut butter
- Bread

DIRECTIONS:
Take the bread then spread honey and peanut butter on it.

Add apple slices as a topping and make it into a sandwich.

Enjoy!

Nutrition: Calories: 300 Total Fat: 16g Total Carbohydrates: 32g Fiber: 4g Sugar: 13g Protein: 11g

67. ICED ESPRESSO LATTE

PREPARATION TIME
5 MIN

COOKING TIME
5 MIN

SERVINGS
2

INGREDIENTS:

- 2 cups, brewed, cooled Decaffeinated Espresso Coffee
- 2 tablespoons Brown Sugar
- 1 1/2 cup Fat-free milk
- 2 tablespoons sugar-free Almond Syrup
- 3 to 4 Ice Cubes
- 1 cup, fat-free Whipped Cream
- Ground Espresso Beans

DIRECTIONS:

Mix brown sugar, espresso, milk, and syrup in a pitcher.

Stir it and refrigerate it till it gets cold.

Add 3 to 4 ice cubes to a glass and pour coffee over it.

Add whipped cream to the drink and sprinkle expresso beans, ground

Nutrition: Calories: 149 Total Fat: 3g Total Carbohydrates: 22g Fiber: 0g Sugar: 22g Protein: 7g

68. MINTY-LIME ICED TEA

PREPARATION TIME
5 MIN

COOKING TIME
5 MIN

SERVINGS
2

INGREDIENTS:

- 1 cup, freshly brewed, cooled Unsweetened Tea
- 2 tablespoons Lime Juice
- 2 tablespoons Fresh Mint Leaves
- 6 to 7 Ice Cubes
- Sugar as per taste

DIRECTIONS:

Add lime juice, iced tea, mint leaves, and ice cubes.

Blend until it gets smooth and frothy.

Pour its liquid into a tall glass and garnish with mint.

Nutrition: Calories: 38 Total Fat: 0g Total Carbohydrates: 9g Fiber: 0g Sugar: 8g Protein: 0g

69. FRUIT SMOOTHIES

PREPARATION TIME
5 MIN

COOKING TIME
5 MIN

SERVINGS
2

INGREDIENTS:

- 1 cup, fat-free Vanilla Frozen Yogurt
- 3/4 cup, fat-free Milk
- 1/4 cup concentrate Frozen Orange Juice

DIRECTIONS:

Mix milk, frozen yogurt, and orange juice in a blender and blend until it gets smooth.

Add some ice into a tall glass and pour the smoothie into it.

Enjoy!

Nutrition: Calories: 160 Total Fat: 2g Total Carbohydrates: 34g Fiber: 3g Sugar: 24g Protein: 5g

70. BERRY SMOOTHIE

PREPARATION TIME
5 MIN

COOKING TIME
5 MIN

SERVINGS
2

INGREDIENTS:

- 1 Banana
- 1/2 cup Strawberries
- 4 tablespoons Lemon Juice
- 1/2 cup Berries – Blueberries or Blackberries
- 2 ounces Fresh Raw Baby Spinach
- Fresh Mint As per taste
- 1 cup Ice or Cold Water

DIRECTIONS:

Prepare a mixer or blender, put all ingredients, and let it blend until it turns into a puree.

Serve in a glass or cup and enjoy.

Nutrition: Calories: 161 Total Fat: 2g Total Carbohydrates: 34g Fiber: 3g Sugar: 24g Protein: 5g

CHAPTER 4. 30 DAYS DASH MEAL PREPARATION PLANS 2021

DAY	BREAKFAST	LUNCH	DINNER	SNACK
1	BACON EGG & SPINACH CASSEROLE	CHICKEN VEGETABLE SOUP	TUSCAN WHITE BEANS WITH SHRIMP, SPINACH, AND FETA	MINI BELL PEPPER LOADED NACHOS
2	BISCUITS AND GRAVY	SALMON AND EDAMAME CAKES	CHICKEN & BROCCOLI IN SESAME NOODLES	ZUCCHINI PIZZA BOATS
3	BREAKFAST TOSTADA	TOFU AND MUSHROOM BURGER	SPICY BAKED POTATOES	FRUIT SKEWERS WITH VANILLA HONEY YOGURT DIP
4	CREAMY BANANA OATMEAL	FLAT BREAD PIZZA	TURKEY STIR FRY WITH VEGETABLES	BAKED PARMESAN ZUCCHINI STICKS
5	EGG SALAD	SHEPHERD'S PIE	TANDOORI CHICKEN	SPINACH ARTICHOKE DIP
6	HOMEMADE BACON	EASY ROASTED SALMON	PEAR QUESADILLAS	BUFFALO CHICKPEA AND ARTICHOKE TAQUITOS
7	OATMEAL PANCAKES	ZUCCHINI PAD THAI	PORCINI MUSHROOMS WITH PASTA	LOADED AVOCADO QUESADILLAS

8	SAUSAGE AND POTATOES MIX	BAKED MACARONI	PORK TENDERLOIN WITH SWEET POTATOES & APPLE	CRUNCHY KALE CHIPS
9	NICE WHEAT MUFFINS	OPEN-FACED GARDEN TUNA SANDWICH	SHRIMP & NECTARINE SALAD	CRISPY PARMESAN RANCH ZUCCHINI CHIPS
10	PUMPKIN VANILLA SMOOTHIE	CURRIED CHICKEN WRAP	CHILI-LIME GRILLED PINEAPPLE	CINNAMON YOGURT FRUIT DIP
11	BUCKWHEAT PANCAKES WITH STRAWBERRIES	SHRIMP WITH PASTA, ARTICHOKE, AND SPINACH	TASTY TORTILLA BAKE	CHOCOLATE YOGURT PUDDING
12	TRIPLE MUFFINS	PISTACHIO CRUSTED HALIBUT WITH SPICY YOGURT	PORK CHOPS WITH TOMATO CURRY	PEANUT BUTTER ENERGY BITES
13	PINEAPPLE POTATO SALAD	VEGGIE SUSHI	PEPPERED SOLE	APPLE PIE OAT BARS
14	BREAKFAST SAUSAGE GRAVY	COBB SALAD	THAI CHICKEN PASTA SKILLET	BAKED CHICKEN NUGGETS
15	PUMPKIN PIE SMOOTHIE DELIGHT	TOFU AND MUSHROOM BURGER	SHRIMP ORZO WITH FETA	CINNAMON APPLES
16	BISQUICK TURKEY BREAKFAST BALLS	AVOCADO SANDWICH WITH LEMON AND CILANTRO	BEEF AND BLUE CHEESE PENNE WITH PESTO	RANCH AND CHEESE BELL PEPPER POPPERS
17	EASY OMELET WAFFLES	CHICKEN VEGETABLE SOUP	CALIFORNIA QUINOA	BAKED CHICKEN TACOS

18	BREAKFAST FRUIT BOWL	SPINACH SALAD WITH WALNUTS AND STRAWBERRY	PEPPERED TUNA KABOBS	SWEET AND SPICY ROASTED SWEET POTATO ROUNDS
19	OATMEAL PANCAKES	FLAT BREAD PIZZA	CHILI-LIME GRILLED PINEAPPLE	CHOCOLATE YOGURT PUDDING
20	HOMEMADE BACON	SALMON AND EDAMAME CAKES	PEPPERED SOLE	PEANUT BUTTER ENERGY BITES
21	EGG SALAD	SHEPHERD'S PIE	SHRIMP & NECTARINE SALAD	CINNAMON YOGURT FRUIT DIP
22	CREAMY BANANA OATMEAL	ROASTED BRUSSELS SPROUTS, CHICKEN, AND POTATOES	PORCINI MUSHROOMS WITH PASTA	CRISPY PARMESAN RANCH ZUCCHINI CHIPS
23	BREAKFAST TOSTADA	PAELLA WITH CHICKEN, LEEKS, AND TARRAGON	PEAR QUESADILLAS	CRUNCHY KALE CHIPS
24	BISCUITS AND GRAVY	PISTACHIO CRUSTED HALIBUT WITH SPICY YOGURT	TASTY TORTILLA BAKE	LOADED AVOCADO QUESADILLAS
25	BACON EGG & SPINACH CASSEROLE	SHRIMP WITH PASTA, ARTICHOKE, AND SPINACH	PORK TENDERLOIN WITH SWEET POTATOES & APPLE	BUFFALO CHICKPEA AND ARTICHOKE TAQUITOS
26	PINEAPPLE POTATO SALAD	EASY ROASTED SALMON	TANDOORI CHICKEN	SPINACH ARTICHOKE DIP
27	TRIPLE MUFFINS	ZUCCHINI PAD THAI	SPICY BAKED POTATOES	BAKED PARMESAN ZUCCHINI STICKS

28	SAUSAGE AND POTATOES MIX	BAKED MACARONI	CHICKEN & BROCCOLI IN SESAME NOODLES	FRUIT SKEWERS WITH VANILLA HONEY YOGURT DIP
29	NICE WHEAT MUFFINS	OPEN-FACED GARDEN TUNA SANDWICH	TUSCAN WHITE BEANS WITH SHRIMP, SPINACH, AND FETA	ZUCCHINI PIZZA BOATS
30	PUMPKIN VANILLA SMOOTHIE	CURRIED CHICKEN WRAP	TURKEY STIR FRY WITH VEGETABLES	MINI BELL PEPPER LOADED NACHOS

BREAKFAST

71. BACON EGG & SPINACH CASSEROLE

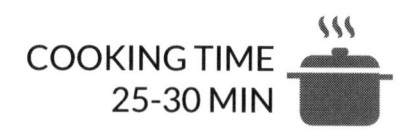

PREPARATION TIME 15 MIN

COOKING TIME 25-30 MIN

SERVINGS 2

INGREDIENTS:

- 1/4 tsp. black pepper
- 1/3 green bell pepper, chopped
- 24 oz. spinach
- 3/4 cup cheddar, shredded
- 1 cup egg white
- 2/3 cup mushrooms, sliced
- 4 slices bacon, low sodium
- 2 tbsp. olive oil, separated
- 1/3 cup red onion, chopped
- olive oil cooking spray
- 1/4 tsp. salt
- 1 large egg
- 1/3 red bell pepper, chopped

DIRECTIONS:

Scrub the bell pepper and mushrooms thoroughly. Chop the bell pepper and slice the mushrooms and set to the side.

Remove the outer skin from the onion and chop into small sections. Set to the side.

Empty one tablespoon of the oil into a pan and arrange the sliced bacon, so they are not touching. Brown for approximately 2 minutes while flipping over as needed to fry to your preferred crispiness.

Transfer to a platter layered with kitchen paper and set to the side to cool.

Adjust your stove to heat at the temperature of 375° Fahrenheit. Apply olive oil to a glass baking dish and set to the side.

Transfer the 3 teaspoons of oil that remains into the skillet and combine the chopped mushrooms, onion, and bell pepper into the pan.

Heat for approximately three minutes. Half of the vegetables should be distributed using a slotted spoon on the prepped baking dish's base.

Layer the spinach over the vegetables and empty the remaining cooked vegetables on top of the spinach.

Use a glass dish to combine the pepper, egg, egg whites, and salt until integrated. Empty the dish on top of the cooked vegetables.

Take the cooked bacon, crush it into small chunks over the eggs, and dust it with the shredded cheese.

Heat in the stove for 20 minutes and remove to the counter.

Wait about a quarter of an hour before serving and enjoy!

Nutrition: Calories: 248 Total Fat: 15g Total Carbohydrates: 8g Fiber: 3g Sugar: 2g Protein: 21g

72. BISCUITS AND GRAVY

PREPARATION TIME 15 MIN
COOKING TIME 25 MIN
SERVINGS 2

INGREDIENTS:

- 1 and 1/4 cups whole wheat flour, separated
- 1/2 tsp. Mrs. Dash's Table Blend, salt-free
- 2 tbsp. olive oil
- 1/4 tsp. black pepper
- 1 oz. margarine
- 1/2 tbsp. baking powder, salt-free
- 1/2 tsp. sugar, granulated
- 1/4 tsp. salt
- 1 and 1/2 cup milk, skim and separated

DIRECTIONS:

Adjust the stove temperature to heat at 425° Fahrenheit. Layer a flat sheet with baking lining and set to the side.

Use a glass dish to blend the baking powder, one cup of the flour, seasoning, margarine, and granulated sugar until there is no more lumpiness present.

Finally, integrate 8 ounces of the milk into the mixture and blend until it becomes a thick dough.

Dust a flat surface with 2 tablespoons of the flour and flatten the pastry to be about one-inch thick.

Get a glass or a cookie cutter that is at least 2 inches in diameter, cut the dough into 6 individual circles.

Arrange on the prepped flat sheet and heat for approximately 14 minutes.

In the meantime, heat the olive oil, pepper, leftover 1/8 cup of flour, the leftover one-half cup of the skim milk, and salt in a skillet.

Warm gently for about 10 minutes as the gravy reduces while occasionally stirring.

Transfer the biscuits from the stove and move them onto individual serving plates.

Slice them in half and drizzle the gravy over the top.

Serve immediately and enjoy!

Nutrition: Calories: 370 Total Fat: 21g Total Carbohydrates: 34g Fiber: 1g Sugar: 2g Protein: 14g

73. BREAKFAST TOSTADA

PREPARATION TIME 15 MIN

COOKING TIME 20-25 MIN

SERVINGS 2

INGREDIENTS:

- 8 corn tortillas, low sodium
- 2 scallions, sliced thinly
- 8 tbsp. cream cheese, low-fat
- 1 tsp. Tabasco hot sauce
- 2 small tomatoes, deseeded and chopped
- 1 medium jalapeno, chopped
- 8 large eggs
- 2 slices Swiss cheese, low sodium
- 3 tbsp. cilantro, chopped
- olive oil cooking spray

DIRECTIONS:

Set your stove to the temperature of 375° Fahrenheit.

Place the jalapeno pepper over the stove burner on the setting of a medium.

Flip the pepper over as it begins to turn black. This should take approximately 2 minutes.

Turn the burner off and move the jalapeno with the tongs to a paper towel for about 5 minutes.

In the meantime, arrange the tortillas onto the rack in the stove so they will not fall through.

Heat for approximately 6 minutes and remove carefully to serving dishes.

Put on a pair of gloves and rub the skin off of the jalapeno and chop finely. Set to the side.

Thoroughly wash the tomatoes and chop the scallions and tomatoes. Set aside.

Blend the cream cheese and Tabasco sauce in a glass dish until the consistency is smooth. Set to the side.

Coat a pan with the oil spray and heat the chopped jalapeno for about 90 seconds.

In a separate dish, whip the eggs and transfer the chopped scallions into the dish.

Empty the eggs into the skillet and occasionally stir the eggs to set for approximately 60 seconds.

Combine the chopped tomatoes and sliced cheese to the skillet and heat for another 2 minutes. Remove from the burner.

Evenly distribute the sour cream to each tortilla, spreading almost to the edges.

Split the egg mixture evenly between each of the tortillas and serve immediately.

Nutrition: Calories: 211 Total Fat: 8g Total Carbohydrates: 22g Fiber: 6g Sugar: 0.6g Protein: 12g

74. CREAMY BANANA OATMEAL

PREPARATION TIME
5 MIN

COOKING TIME
10 MIN

SERVINGS
2

INGREDIENTS:

- 1 cup of berries of choice
- 2 cups oats, old fashioned
- 1 and 1/3 cup almonds, sliced
- 3 and 1/4 cups water
- 1 tbsp. ground cinnamon
- 2 medium bananas

DIRECTIONS:

Crush the bananas thoroughly until smooth.

Empty the water into a saucepan and incorporate the mashed banana.

Combine the oats in the pan and heat until the water bubbles.

Adjust the temperature of the burner to low and continue to warm for approximately 7 minutes.

Remove from heat and top with the ground cinnamon, berries, and sliced almonds.

Serve immediately and enjoy!

Nutrition: Calories: 265 Total Fat: 3g Total Carbohydrates: 47g Fiber: 5g Sugar: 0g Protein: 15g

75. EGG SALAD

PREPARATION TIME 10 MIN

COOKING TIME 15 MIN

SERVINGS 2

INGREDIENTS:

- 1 and 1/2 cups pre-packaged salad greens
- 1/8-cup mozzarella cheese
- 1 cup sweet bell pepper of your choice, chopped
- 1/4 tsp. black pepper
- 1 tbsp. avocado, diced
- 2 large eggs
- 3/4 cup tomato, chopped
- 1/4 tsp. salt
- 8 cups cold water, separated
- 1 tsp. thyme, crushed
- 1/2 cup cucumber, sliced
- 1 tsp. olive oil

DIRECTIONS:

Empty 4 cups of the cold water into a stockpot with the eggs and turn the burner on.

When the water starts to bubble, set a timer for 7 minutes.

Meanwhile, scrub and chop the tomato, cucumber, avocado, and bell pepper and transfer to a salad dish.

After the timer has chimed, remove the hot water and empty the remaining 4 cups of cold water on top of the eggs. Set aside for approximately 5 minutes.

Peel the shell once cooled and dice into small sections then transfer to the dish.

Combine the salad greens and shredded mozzarella cheese to the salad dish and turn until integrated with the vegetables.

Dispense the olive oil over the dish and blend the crushed thyme, pepper, and salt until mixed well.

Serve immediately and enjoy!

Nutrition: Calories: 200 Total Fat: 18g Total Carbohydrates: 3g Fiber: 0g Sugar: 0g Protein: 10g

76. HOMEMADE BACON

PREPARATION TIME 10 MIN

COOKING TIME 30 MIN

SERVINGS 2

INGREDIENTS:

- 1 tsp. cumin seasoning
- 1 tsp. black pepper
- 2 tbsp. olive oil
- 16 oz. pork belly, sliced no more than 1/4 inch thick
- 4 tsp. liquid smoke
- 2 tsp. smoked paprika seasoning
- 3 tbsp. maple syrup
- 1/4 tsp. salt

DIRECTIONS:

Set your stove to the temperature of 200° Fahrenheit. Cover a flat sheet with a rim with foil. Set to the side.

Remove the rind from the pork belly slices by using kitchen scissors and arrange the slices on the prepped baking pan, so they are in a single layer and not touching.

Utilize another pan if necessary, depending on the thickness of your bacon.

In a glass dish, blend the maple syrup and the liquid smoke until integrated.

In a separate dish, combine the pepper, cumin, and smoked paprika fully.

Use a pastry brush to apply the maple syrup to each of the bacon slices.

Turn the slices over and repeat step 5.

Dust all of the slices with the mixed seasonings and rub the spices into the meat.

Empty the olive oil into a skillet and arrange the slices in a single layer. You will need to cook in stages.

Brown for approximately 2 minutes while turning over as needed to fry to your desired crispiness fully.

Arrange to the plate and enjoy while hot!

Nutrition: Calories: 145 Total Fat: 15g Total Carbohydrates: 0g Fiber: 0g Sugar: 0g Protein: 3g

77. OATMEAL PANCAKES

PREPARATION TIME 10 MIN

COOKING TIME 20 MIN

SERVINGS 2

INGREDIENTS:

- 1/2 tsp. ground cinnamon
- 4 oz. whole wheat flour
- 2 oz. oats, old fashioned
- 1 tsp. baking powder, salt-free
- 1/8 tsp. salt
- olive oil cooking spray
- 4 oz. milk, skim
- 1/8-cup Greek yogurt, no-fat
- 1 large egg
- 1/2 tsp. vanilla extract
- 3 tsp. brown sugar

DIRECTIONS:

In a big dish, blend the salt, whole wheat flour, ground cinnamon, and whole oats, and baking powder, combine completely.

Using another dish, fully integrate the milk and egg until the mixed well.

Combine the vanilla extract, yogurt, and brown sugar into the eggs and whisk to remove any lumpiness.

Slowly empty the egg dish into the flour dish, making sure it is combined but do not mix too thoroughly.

Warm a skillet. Make sure the skillet is sprayed with olive oil.

Distribute approximately a quarter of the batter into the skillet.

Turn the pancake over after the top starts to bubble after about 60 seconds.

Let the pancake cook for approximately another minute and flip as needed until browned completely.

Remove to a plate and coat the skillet with an additional coat of olive oil spray.

Repeat until all the pancakes are finished.

Serve while hot and enjoy!

Nutrition: Calories: 196 Total Fat: 2g Total Carbohydrates: 32g Fiber: 4g Sugar: 2g Protein: 10g

78. SAUSAGE AND POTATOES MIX

PREPARATION TIME 10 MIN

COOKING TIME 22 MIN

SERVINGS 2

INGREDIENTS:

- 1/2-pound smoked sausage, cooked and chopped
- 3 tablespoons olive oil
- 3/4-pounds red potatoes, cubed
- yellow onions, chopped
- 1 teaspoon thyme, dried
- 2 teaspoons cumin, ground
- A pinch of black pepper

DIRECTIONS:

Warm-up a pan using the oil over medium-high heat, add potatoes and onions, stir and cook for 12 minutes.

Supply sausage, thyme, cumin, and black pepper, stir, cook for 10 minutes more, divide between plates and serve for lunch.

Enjoy!

Nutrition: Calories: 199 Total Fat: 2g Total Carbohydrates: 14g Fiber: 4g Sugar: 0g Protein: 8g

79. NICE WHEAT MUFFINS

PREPARATION TIME 10 MIN

COOKING TIME 25 MIN

SERVINGS 2

INGREDIENTS:

- cooking spray
- 2 cups whole wheat flour
- 1/2 cup of sugar
- 3 1/2 tsps. baking powder
- 2 egg whites
- 3 Tbsps. canola oil
- 1/3 cups fat-free milk
- Tbsp. white vinegar (add this towards the nonfat milk and stir well)
- Optional: 1 cup blueberries, fresh or frozen

DIRECTIONS:

Preheat the oven to 350°F.

Insert paper lines right into a muffin tray.

Place the flour, baking powder, sugar within a bowl, and mix well.

If the blueberries should be added, fold the fruits into the batter since it will avoid the fruits engaging in the bowl's bottom. Leave aside.

In another bowl, mix in the total amount of ingredients.

Fold the flour mixture, combine well without over-mixing.

Fold the batter into the muffin cups and place it within the oven.

Bake for approximately 25 minutes before muffins are well cooked.

Nutrition: Calories: 134 Total Fat: 1.4g Total Carbohydrates: 27g Fiber: 4g Sugar: 5g Protein: 6g

80. PUMPKIN VANILLA SMOOTHIE

PREPARATION TIME: 5 MIN
COOKING TIME: 5 MIN
SERVINGS: 2

INGREDIENTS:

- cup milk
- Tbsps. unsweetened instant tea (optional)
- 1/2 tsp. pumpkin pie spice
- 1/4 tsp. ground cardamom
- 1 banana
- 3/4 cup fat-free vanilla yogurt
- 1/2 cup canned pumpkin
- 1 Tbsp. pure maple syrup
- 1 cup ice (about 10 cubes)

DIRECTIONS:

Place the moment tea as well as the spices inside a food processor.

Mix inside the milk and process before tea is well dissolved.

Toss in the total amount ingredients, excluding the ice and blend until smooth.

Depending on the thickness, continue adding ice to find you in the right consistency.

Transfer the mixture into individual glasses and serve.

Nutrition: Calories: 175 Total Fat: 0g Total Carbohydrates: 15g Fiber: 5g Sugar: 7g Protein: 23g

81. PUMPKIN PIE SMOOTHIE DELIGHT

PREPARATION TIME 5 MIN

COOKING TIME 5 MIN

SERVINGS 2

INGREDIENTS:

- scoop vanilla whey protein
- 1/4 cup 100% pumpkin purees (NOT pie filling!)
- 1/8 cup Splenda granular
- 1 Dash salt (I take advantage of Morton's Lite Salt)
- pumpkin pie spice, to taste
- 1 cup of soy milk
- Tbsps. Fat-Free Cool Whip
- 4-5 ice, if desired

DIRECTIONS:

Place all ingredients inside a food processor.

Add all the ingredients, and then mix until smooth.

Add the ice, if required.

Nutrition: Calories: 150 Total Fat: 2g Total Carbohydrates: 28g Fiber: 6g Sugar: 6g Protein: 15g

82. BUCKWHEAT PANCAKES WITH STRAWBERRIES

PREPARATION TIME 5 MIN
COOKING TIME 15 MIN
SERVINGS 2

INGREDIENTS:

- 2 Egg whites
- tablespoon Olive oil
- 1/2 cup Fat-free milk
- 1/2 cup All-purpose flour
- 1/2 cup Buckwheat flour
- 1 tablespoon Baking powder
- 1/2 cup Sparkling normal water
- 2 cups sliced Fresh strawberries

DIRECTIONS:

Mix the egg whites, olive oil, and milk in a big bowl.

In another bowl combine the all-purpose flour, buckwheat flour, and baking powder and mix thoroughly.

Slowly add the dry ingredients towards the egg white mixture while you alternately add the dazzling water. Be sure to mix between each addition until all the ingredients combine right into a batter.

Warm a non-stick frying pan on medium heat. Spoon 1/2 cup of the pancake batter into the pan.

Cook before top surface in the pancake bubbles plus the edges turns lightly brown, about 2 minutes.

Flip and cook before the bottom is nicely brown and cooked through, one to two minutes longer.

Repeat with the other pancake batter.

Transfer the pancakes to individual plates. Top each with 1/2 cup sliced strawberries. Serve.

Nutrition: Calories: 142 Total Fat: 3g Total Carbohydrates: 25g Fiber: 4g Sugar: 6g Protein: 6g

83. TRIPLE MUFFINS

PREPARATION TIME
10 MIN

COOKING TIME
25 MIN

SERVINGS
2

INGREDIENTS:

- non-stick cooking spray
- 1-1/3 cups all-purpose flour
- 3/4 cup buckwheat flour
- 1/4 to 1/3 cup sugar
- 1-1/2 tsp. baking powder
- 1 tsp. ground cinnamon
- 1/2 tsp. baking soda
- 1/2 tsp. salt
- 2 eggs, slightly beaten
- 1 cup mashed cooked butternut squash
- 1/2 cup fat-free milk
- 2 Tbsps. cooking oil
- 1/2 tsp. finely shredded orange peel
- 1/4 cup orange juice
- 3/4 cup fresh or frozen blueberries
- Rolled oats

DIRECTIONS:

Preheat the oven to 400°F.

Insert paper liners right into a 12 x 2 1/2-inches muffin cups and leave aside.

Add the flours, baking powder, baking soda, sugar, and salt in a mixing bowl. Mix well.

Dig a proper in the center of the mixture and keep aside for some time.

Mix the eggs milk, squash, oil, orange juice, plus the peel in another bowl.

Put the flour mixture into the egg mixture and mix until moist.

Mix inside the blueberries.

Fold the batter mixture into the lined muffin cups and top up each cup with oats.

Bake for approximately 20 minutes before muffins certainly are a light brown.

Allow cooling for 5-6 minutes.

Take right out of the muffin cups and serve.

84. PINEAPPLE POTATO SALAD

PREPARATION TIME 10 MIN

COOKING TIME 30 MIN

SERVINGS 2

INGREDIENTS:
- 2 cups pineapple, peeled and cubed
- 4 sweet potatoes, cubed
- tablespoon olive oil
- 1/4 cup coconut, unsweetened and shredded
- 1/3 cup almonds, chopped
- 1 cup coconut cream

DIRECTIONS:

Arrange sweet potatoes on the lined baking sheet, add the olive oil.

Introduce within the oven at 350°F.

Roast for 30 minutes; put them in a salad bowl.

Add coconut, pineapple, almonds, and cream, toss.

Split between plates and serve as a side dish. Enjoy!

Nutrition: Calories: 150 Total Fat: 0.3g Total Carbohydrates: 36g Fiber: 3g Sugar: 14g Protein: 2g

85. BREAKFAST SAUSAGE GRAVY

PREPARATION TIME
5 MIN

COOKING TIME
15 MIN

SERVINGS
2

INGREDIENTS:

- 1/2 lb. ground breakfast sausage
- 1/4 cup all-purpose flour
- 3 cups of milk
- Salt
- Pepper

DIRECTIONS:

Place the bottom breakfast sausages on the non-stick skillet.

Leave for approximately 7-8 minutes until they may be well browned.

Contribute the flour, milk, salt, pepper, and stir well.

Let the mixture boil and thicken for some time.

Lower heat and leave for 4-5 minutes.

Serve.

Nutrition: Calories: 138 Total Fat: 8g Total Carbohydrates: 7g Fiber: 0g Sugar: 3g Protein: 8g

86. BISQUICK TURKEY BREAKFAST BALLS

PREPARATION TIME
5 MIN

COOKING TIME
25-30 MIN

SERVINGS
2

INGREDIENTS:

- 16 oz. cheddar 2%
- 3 cups heart healthy Bisquick
- 16 oz. low sodium turkey breakfast sausage
- 1/3 cup milk

DIRECTIONS:

Preheat an oven to 375°F.

Place all ingredients within a bowl.

Add more Bisquick if the mixture is too sticky.

Form little round balls and put on a cookie sheet.

Bake for approximately quarter-hour until cooked.

Allow to cool and serve.

Nutrition: Calories: 224 Total Fat: 5g Total Carbohydrates: 16g Fiber: 11g Sugar: 2g Protein: 14g

87. EASY OMELET WAFFLES

PREPARATION TIME 10 MIN

COOKING TIME 5 MIN

SERVINGS 2

INGREDIENTS:

- 4 eggs
- A pinch of black pepper
- 2 tablespoons ham, chopped
- 1/4 cup low-fat cheddar, shredded
- 2 tablespoons parsley, chopped
- Cooking spray

DIRECTIONS:

Within a bowl, combine the eggs with pepper, ham, cheese, and parsley and whisk effectively.

Grease your waffle iron with cooking spray, add the egg mix, cook for 4-5 minutes.

Divide the waffles between plates and serve them for breakfast.

Enjoy!

Nutrition: Calories: 200 Total Fat: 7g Total Carbohydrates: 29g Fiber: 3g Sugar: 0g Protein: 3g

88. BREAKFAST FRUIT BOWL

PREPARATION TIME
5 MIN

COOKING TIME
5 MIN

SERVINGS
2

INGREDIENTS:
- cup mango, chopped
- 1 banana, sliced
- 1 cup pineapple, chopped
- 1 cup almond milk

DIRECTIONS:
Prepare a bowl, combine the mango using the banana, pineapple, and almond milk.

Stir, divide into smaller bowls, and serve breakfast.

Enjoy!

Nutrition: Calories: 103 Total Fat: 0g Total Carbohydrates: 25g Fiber: 0g Sugar: 0g Protein: 1g

LUNCH

89. CURRIED CHICKEN WRAP

PREPARATION TIME
10 MIN

COOKING TIME
10 MIN

SERVINGS
2

INGREDIENTS:
- 2 medium whole-wheat tortilla
- 1/3 cup cooked chicken, chopped
- 1 cup apple, chopped
- 1 tablespoon light mayonnaise
- 1 teaspoon curry powder
- 1 cup, or about 15, raw baby carrots

DIRECTIONS:
Mix together all the ingredients except tortillas.

Divide and place at the center of the tortillas.

Roll and serve.

Nutrition: Calories: 380 Total Fat: 9g Total Carbohydrates: 47g Fiber: 4g Sugar: 5g Protein: 27g

90. OPEN-FACED GARDEN TUNA SANDWICH

PREPARATION TIME 10 MIN

COOKING TIME 15 MIN

SERVINGS 2

INGREDIENTS:

- 2 cans (5 ounces each) low sodium tuna packed in water, drained
- 4 green onions, sliced
- 4 slices hearty multigrain bread
- 1 tablespoon fresh parsley, chopped
- 1 tablespoon lemon juice
- 1 tablespoon extra-virgin olive oil
- 1/4 cup cherry tomatoes, sliced
- A handful of fresh arugulas
- 2 tablespoons low fat whipped cream cheese
- Black pepper powder to taste

DIRECTIONS:

Mix together oil, lemon juice, parsley, green onion, and pepper.

Add tuna to a bowl. Add about 2/3 of the above mixture and mix well.

Spread a little of the remaining mixture lightly on both sides of the bread.

Heat a nonstick pan over high heat. Place the bread slices and cook until the bottom side is golden brown. Turn and cook the other side.

Add the remaining mixture to the arugula and toss well.

To make sandwiches: Spread cream cheese on each of the bread slices.

Divide and spread the tuna mixture over the slices. Place the arugula over the tuna mixture and finally cherry tomatoes.

Nutrition: Calories: 360 Total Fat: 20g Total Carbohydrates: 18g Fiber: 5g Sugar: 5g Protein: 24g

91. BAKED MACARONI

PREPARATION TIME 10 MIN

COOKING TIME 30 MIN

SERVINGS 2

INGREDIENTS:

- 1-pound extra-lean ground beef
- 2 large onion, diced
- 2 boxes (7 ounces each) whole-wheat elbow macaroni, cooked according to instructions on the package
- 2 jars (15 ounces each) low sodium spaghetti sauce
- 3/4 cup Parmesan cheese

DIRECTIONS:

Prepare a large nonstick pan over medium heat. Add onions and sauté for a few minutes until the onions are translucent.

Add beef and cook until brown. Add pasta and spaghetti sauce. Mix well and transfer into a greased baking dish.

Bake in a preheated oven at 350 degrees F for about 30 minutes.

Serve garnished with Parmesan cheese.

Nutrition: Calories: 200 Total Fat: 7g Total Carbohydrates: 25g Fiber: 0g Sugar: 3g Protein: 4g

92. ZUCCHINI PAD THAI

PREPARATION TIME 15 MIN
COOKING TIME 30 MIN
SERVINGS 2

INGREDIENTS:

For the sauce:
- 3/4 tablespoon coconut sugar
- 1 teaspoon Sriracha sauce or to taste
- 2 tablespoons tamarind paste
- 2 teaspoons low sodium tamari
- 1 tablespoon lime juice
- 2 tablespoons low sodium chicken stock

For the noodles:
- large carrot, peeled, trimmed with top and bottom sliced off
- 2 large zucchinis, trimmed with top and bottom sliced off

For Pad Thai:
- 1/2 cups bean sprouts
- 1 large skinless, boneless chicken breast, sliced
- 1 egg, beaten
- 2 teaspoons olive oil, divided
- 1 green onion, thinly sliced
- 2 tablespoons peanuts, finely chopped
- Lime wedges to serve
- Salt to taste
- Pepper powder to taste

DIRECTIONS:

To make noodles: Make noodles of the carrot and zucchini using a spiralizer or a julienne peeler.

For pad Thai: Place a nonstick pan over medium heat. Add 1/2-teaspoon oil. When the oil is heated, add egg, salt, and pepper. Keep stirring to scramble it. Remove from the pan when cooked and place it in a bowl.

Put oil in a warm nonstick pan. Once heated, add chicken breasts, salt, and pepper.

Cook until the chicken is tender inside and golden-brown outside. Place it along with the egg.

To make the sauce: Add all the ingredients of the sauce to a bowl and mix well. Place the pan back on the heat. Put the sauce mixture into the pan and cook until it is bubbly.

Add zucchini and carrot noodles and cook sauté for a few minutes until it is thoroughly heated and slightly softened.

Add chicken, eggs, and sprouts. Mix well and heat thoroughly.

Garnish with lemon wedges, green onion, and peanuts and serve immediately.

Nutrition: Calories: 224 Total Fat: 3g Total Carbohydrates: 12g Fiber: 6g Sugar: 10g Protein: 11g

93. EASY ROASTED SALMON

PREPARATION TIME 5 MIN

COOKING TIME 25 MIN

SERVINGS 2

INGREDIENTS:

- 8 (6 ounces each) wild salmon fillets
- 2 lemons, cut into 8 wedges
- Freshly ground black pepper to taste
- 1/2 cup fresh dill, minced
- 8 cloves garlic, peeled and minced

DIRECTIONS:

Lay the salmon fillets in a large greased baking dish. Sprinkle lemon juice, pepper, dill, and garlic.

Prepare the oven at 400 degrees F then place the dish and bake for about 20-25 minutes until the salmon is opaque.

Serve immediately.

Nutrition: Calories: 240 Total Fat: 14g Total Carbohydrates: 0g Fiber: 0g Sugar: 0g Protein: 28g

94. Shrimp with Pasta, Artichoke, and Spinach

PREPARATION TIME 10 MIN

COOKING TIME 30 MIN

SERVINGS 2

INGREDIENTS:

- 1 tablespoon grapeseed oil
- 1 medium onion, diced small
- 1/2 cup mushrooms, thinly sliced
- 2 garlic cloves, thinly sliced
- 1/2 cup canned artichokes, quartered
- 1/2 cups chicken broth
- 6-ounce raw angel hair pasta, broken in half
- 1/2 cup raw shrimps, peeled, deveined
- 1/2 teaspoon dried oregano
- 1/2 cup fresh spinach roughly chopped
- Salt to taste
- Pepper to taste

Optional:
- A pinch of crushed red pepper flakes

DIRECTIONS:

Place a pot with oil over medium heat. When the oil is heated, add onions, mushrooms, and garlic.

Sauté for a couple of minutes and add artichokes, chicken broth, pasta, shrimps, oregano, red pepper flakes, salt, and pepper.

Mix well and bring to a boil. Put cover and cook until the pasta is al dente.

Add spinach and cook for a couple of minutes until the spinach wilts.

Adjust the seasonings if required. Serve hot.

Nutrition: Calories: 500 Total Fat: 18g Total Carbohydrates: 56g Fiber: 12g Sugar: 0g Protein: 30g

95. PISTACHIO CRUSTED HALIBUT WITH SPICY YOGURT

PREPARATION TIME 15 MIN

COOKING TIME 30 MIN

SERVINGS 2

INGREDIENTS:

For Halibut
- 6 (1 1/4-inch-thick) pieces skinless halibut fillet of about 6 ounces each
- 1/2 cup shelled pistachio nuts (chopped)
- 1/2 cups whole milk
- 1/3 cup extra virgin olive oil
- 4 1/2 tablespoons cornmeal
- 1/2 tsp. black pepper powder (to taste)

For spicy yogurt:
- 1/2 cups thick Greek yogurt
- 1 cup cucumber, peeled, finely chopped
- 1 medium onion, finely chopped
- tablespoons fresh dill, chopped
- tablespoons lemon juice
- teaspoons dried Maras pepper
- 3/4 teaspoon salt

DIRECTIONS:

Place fish in a baking dish. Pour milk all over the fish. Put cover and refrigerate about 30 minutes.

Meanwhile, mix in shallow bowl pistachio nuts and cornmeal.

Get the fish with a slotted spoon and place on a plate. Season with salt and pepper. Coat the fish pieces with cornmeal mixture and place them on another plate.

Place a heavy skillet over medium-high heat. Add oil. When the oil is heated, place the fish pieces in it. When the underside is golden, flip sides and cook the other side of the fish until golden brown.

Meanwhile make the spicy yogurt as follows: Mix all the Ingredients of spicy yogurt and set aside.

Serve fried fish with spicy yogurt.

Nutrition: Calories: 232 Total Fat: 8g Total Carbohydrates: 5g Fiber: 0g Sugar: 0g Protein: 31g

96. PAELLA WITH CHICKEN, LEEKS, AND TARRAGON

PREPARATION TIME 15 MIN

COOKING TIME 20 MIN

SERVINGS 2

INGREDIENTS:

- 2 teaspoons extra-virgin olive oil
- large onion, sliced
- 4 leeks (whites only), thinly sliced
- 6 -7 garlic cloves, minced
- pounds chicken breast, boneless, skinless, cut into strips of 1/2 inch wide and 2 inches long
- large tomatoes, chopped
- 1 red pepper, sliced
- 1 green pepper, sliced
- 1 1/3 cups long-grain brown rice
- 2 teaspoons tarragon, or to taste
- cups fat-free, unsalted chicken broth
- 2 cups frozen peas
- 1/2 cup chopped fresh parsley
- 2 lemon, cut into 4 wedges each

DIRECTIONS:

Put olive oil in a skillet with medium temperature. Once heated, sauté onions, garlic, leeks, and chicken for a few minutes or until the onions are translucent and the chicken is light brown.

Add tomatoes, peppers, and sauté for 4-5 minutes.

Add rice, tarragon, and broth. Mix well.

When it boils, lower heat, cover, and simmer for about 12-15 minutes.

Uncover and add peas. Wait for it to simmer or until all the moisture is absorbed and rice is cooked.

Sprinkle parsley and serve with lemon wedges.

Nutrition: Calories: 378 Total Fat: 6g Total Carbohydrates: 46g Fiber: 7g Sugar: 0g Protein: 35g

97. ROASTED BRUSSELS SPROUTS, CHICKEN, AND POTATOES

PREPARATION TIME 10 MIN

COOKING TIME 20 MIN

SERVINGS 2

INGREDIENTS:

- 1/2-pound chicken breasts, boneless, skinless, cut into 2 pieces
- 1/2 cups Yukon gold potatoes or red potatoes, cut into bite-sized pieces
- cups Brussels sprouts, trimmed, quartered
- 1/2 cup onions, diced
- 1/4 cup vinaigrette dressing
- 1 tablespoon lemon juice
- 1/4 teaspoon garlic salt
- 1 teaspoon dried oregano
- 1 teaspoon Dijon mustard
- 2 tablespoons kalamata olives, quartered
- Freshly ground black pepper to taste
- Cooking spray

DIRECTIONS:

Grease a baking sheet with cooking spray.

Place the chicken pieces, Brussels sprouts, potatoes, and onions in a large bowl.

Mix together in a small bowl: vinaigrette, lemon juice, mustard, oregano, pepper, olives, and garlic salt and put vegetables in the bowl.

Transfer the contents to the baking sheet.

Bake in a warm oven at 400 degrees F for 20 minutes or until the chicken and potatoes are tender.

Stir in between a couple of times.

Remove from the oven. Mix well and serve.

Nutrition: Calories: 361 Total Fat: 10g Total Carbohydrates: 37g Fiber: 7g Sugar: 0g Protein: 32g

98. SHEPHERD'S PIE

PREPARATION TIME 10 MIN

COOKING TIME 30 MIN

SERVINGS 2

INGREDIENTS:
- large baking potato, peeled, diced
- 1/4 cup low-fat milk
- 1/2-pound lean ground beef
- 1 medium onion, chopped
- cloves garlic, minced
- 1 tablespoon flour
- cups of frozen mixed vegetables
- 1/2 cup low sodium beef broth
- 1/2 cup cheddar cheese, sliced
- Pepper powder to taste

DIRECTIONS:

Prepare a saucepan covered with water then put the potatoes. Cook until the potatoes are done. Drain and mash the potatoes.

Add milk to the mashed potatoes and mix well. Keep aside

Place a skillet over medium heat. Add onion, garlic, and beef. Cook until the beef is browned.

Add vegetables and broth. Heat thoroughly.

Transfer to a baking dish. Spread the potato mixture over this.

Sprinkle cheese on top.

Bake in a warm oven at 375 degrees for 25-30 minutes or until the cheese is lightly browned.

Nutrition: Calories: 420 Total Fat: 21g Total Carbohydrates: 29g Fiber: 3g Sugar: 5g Protein: 28g

99. SALMON AND EDAMAME CAKES

PREPARATION TIME
10 MIN

COOKING TIME
30 MIN

SERVINGS
2

INGREDIENTS:

- 4 cups flaked, cooked salmon
- cup frozen edamame, thawed
- 4 large egg whites
- 1/2 cup whole-wheat panko breadcrumbs (Japanese breadcrumbs)
- scallions, finely chopped
- tablespoons fresh ginger, peeled, minced
- 2 cloves garlic, crushed
- 2 tablespoons cilantro, finely chopped
- Canola oil cooking spray
- Lime wedges to serve

DIRECTIONS:

Add all the Ingredients except lime wedges to a bowl and mix well.

Divide the mixture into 8-10 balls and shape them into cakes.

Arrange the cakes on a wax paper-lined plate. Refrigerate the cakes for about 30 minutes.

Place a nonstick skillet over medium heat. Spray with cooking spray. When the skillet is heated, place the cakes 3-4 cakes.

Cook until the underside is golden brown. Flip and cook the other side.

Serve hot with lemon wedges and a dip of your choice.

Nutrition: Calories: 267 Total Fat: 13g Total Carbohydrates: 5g Fiber: 1g Sugar: 0g Protein: 21g

100. FLAT BREAD PIZZA

PREPARATION TIME
5 MIN

COOKING TIME
20 MIN

SERVINGS
2

INGREDIENTS:

- tbsp of olive oil, plus topping if needed
- flatbread dough (use the whole-grain dough while on a DASH diet)
- 1/2 tsp of dried herbs, red pepper flakes, or other needed spices
- 1 bunch of fresh broccoli, cauliflower, arugula, or other leafy greens vegetables
- 1 bell pepper, diced

DIRECTIONS:

Set the grill to medium heat and brush a thin oil layer.

Cook the flatbread dough on both sides until golden brown, about 2 minutes on either side.

Top flatbread with freshly sliced vegetables and green vegetables. Season to taste, using olive oil, salt, pepper, red pepper flakes, or herbs.

To finish cooking, relocate flatbread pizza to the oven.

Nutrition: Calories: 130 Total Fat: 1g Total Carbohydrates: 25g Fiber: 0g Sugar: 2g Protein: 5g

101. SPINACH SALAD WITH WALNUTS AND STRAWBERRY

PREPARATION TIME 10 MIN

COOKING TIME 15 MIN

SERVINGS 2

INGREDIENTS:

- 1/2 cup walnuts
- 4 cups of fresh spinach, loosely trimmed stems
- 3 tbsp of honey
- 2 tbsp of spicy brown mustard
- 1/4 cup of balsamic vinegar
- 1/4 tsp of sea salt
- 1/4 cup of crumbled feta (about 1 oz), optional

DIRECTIONS:

Heat the oven until 375 ° F.

Arrange walnuts on a rimmed baking sheet and bake for 8 minutes, until they are fragrant and toasted. Switch to a cool plate.

Place the spinach in a large container. The honey, mustard, vinegar, and salt are whisked together in a small cup.

Drizzle the salad over 3/4 of the dressing and scatter the walnuts on top.

Serve sprinkled with both the cheese (if it is used) and the remaining side dressing.

Nutrition: Calories: 129 Total Fat: 8g Total Carbohydrates: 10g Fiber: 3g Sugar: 0.8g Protein: 6.6g

102. CHICKEN VEGETABLE SOUP

PREPARATION TIME
5 MIN

COOKING TIME
10-15 MIN

SERVINGS
2

INGREDIENTS:

- 2 tbsp. of olive oil
- 3 garlic cloves
- onion
- 4 cups of low sodium chicken broth
- 1/2 cup of carrot, sliced
- 1/2 cup of a parsnip, sliced
- cups of a green collar, minced
- can of black beans, drained
- 1/2 cup of seaweed (optional)

DIRECTIONS:

Simmer in the olive oil, garlic, and onion blended.

Pour the broth and vegetables into the chicken and turn to a boil. Switch to a simmer when boiling.

Keep on simmer until the vegetables are soft.

Pour in the strained canned beans and optional seaweed when 5 minutes left to cook.

Nutrition: Calories: 120 Total Fat: 4g Total Carbohydrates: 11g Fiber: 2g Sugar: 4g Protein: 10g

103. AVOCADO SANDWICH WITH LEMON AND CILANTRO

PREPARATION TIME
10 MIN

COOKING TIME
10 MIN

SERVINGS
2

INGREDIENTS:

- medium Hass avocado
- slices of 100% whole wheat bread
- 1/2 cup spinach
- 1/4 cup cilantro
- 1/2 carrots
- 1/4 cup cucumber
- 1/4 cup blueberries
- 1/4 cup red cherries
- tbsp lemon juice
- 1 cup skim milk

DIRECTIONS:

Toast the bread.

Slice the avocado (or as desired) into thin strips and put on toast.

Slice the vegetables, then put them on toast.

Sprinkle with a splash of salt and lemon juice.

Prepare the fruit and enjoy a bowl of mixed fruit on the side with skim milk.

Nutrition: Calories: 580 Total Fat: 31g Total Carbohydrates: 50g Fiber: 4g Sugar: 0g Protein: 9g

104. TOFU AND MUSHROOM BURGER

PREPARATION TIME 10 MIN

COOKING TIME 15 MIN

SERVINGS 2

INGREDIENTS:

- 6 oz solid tofu
- 4 oz mushrooms
- medium onion, chopped
- medium red onion, chopped
- cloves of garlic, minced
- medium tomatoes, diced
- oz cheese (your preference)
- 1 oz coriander, cut
- 1 chili, finely grated
- 1 egg, beaten
- 1 tbsp of flour
- 1 tbsp of canola oil
- whole-wheat hamburger buns
- salt and pepper, to taste
- lettuce
- ketchup
- 1 tbsp of flour
- 4 tbsp of canola oil

DIRECTIONS:

Preheat oven to 275 degrees F.

Sauté the onions, garlic, chili, and mushrooms in a saucepan under medium-high heat. Put it aside.

Then add the tofu, mushrooms, cilantro, and mash together with a fork in a pot.

Add the flour and the egg and blend well in a malleable consistency. Shape into the patties.

Fry patties on both sides in a pan under medium heat, until golden brown. Put it in the oven for 5 minutes.

Place the cheese on the burgers, turn off the oven, and allow the cheese to melt over the burger. Serve, and have fun!

Nutrition: Calories: 400 Total Fat: 12g Total Carbohydrates: 60g Fiber: 5g Sugar: 0g Protein: 16g

105. COBB SALAD

PREPARATION TIME 10 MIN

COOKING TIME 15-20 MIN

SERVINGS 2

INGREDIENTS:

- 2 tbsp extra virgin olive oil
- 2 skinless, boneless breast chicken halves (about 1 lb.), pounded thin with a meat tenderizer instrument
- 1/4 cup leftover roasted turkey breast
- head roman lettuce, sliced, rinsed and spin-dried
- small bunch of frisée or your choice of lettuce if not available, divided, washed, and spun dry
- 1 medium avocado, pitted, peeled, and chopped
- large eggs, hard-boiled and chopped into circles
- tbsp chopped mustard seed
- 1 tbsp sliced fresh chives
- 1 tbsp freshly squeezed lemon juice
- freshly chopped black pepper (optional)

DIRECTIONS:

Warm the cooking oil over medium heat in a cast-iron skillet.

Pat the chicken breasts with paper towels and cook for 6 to 8 minutes, flipping halfway through. Test an internal temperature of 160° F with an instant-read thermometer. Remove from heat, arrange on a plate, cover with foil loosely, and put aside.

Attach the diced turkey to the same pan and cook for 2 to 3 minutes, just enough to crisp. Remove the paper towels from the heat and rinse.

Combine the romaine then frisée, then put on two wide plates equally. Slice the chicken, then place it on top.

Arrange the turkey, avocado, tomato, and chopped eggs over the lettuce in orderly rows.

The lemon juice, mustard seed, and chives are mixed in a small cup. Put the glaze on top of the salad, if needed, supplemented with pepper.

Nutrition: Calories: 400 Total Fat: 28g Total Carbohydrates: 12g Fiber: 5g Sugar: 4g Protein: 30g

PREPARATION TIME
10 MIN

COOKING TIME
15 MIN

SERVINGS
2

106. VEGGIE SUSHI

INGREDIENTS:

- 3 cups of brown rice
- 2 tbsp of rice wine vinegar
- 2 avocados, longitudinally cut
- 2 carrots, longitudinally sliced
- cucumber, longitudinally sliced
- Ponzu sauce, to taste

DIRECTIONS:

Cook brown rice, as indicated in instructions. Fold rice to vinegar rice wine. Let the cooked rice cool down.

When cool, spread rice uniformly with a wooden spoon on a bamboo sushi mat, or dip your hands in a cold bowl of water and spread the rice with your fingertips, on top layer avocado, cabbage, and slices of cucumber.

Using the mat to roll it into a packed roll of rice and vegetable, slide the mat out and repeat.

Slice into circles of 1/2 inch. Serve.

Nutrition: Calories: 135 Total Fat: 3g Total Carbohydrates: 22g Fiber: 2g Sugar: 5g Protein: 3g

DINNER

107. TURKEY STIR FRY WITH VEGETABLES

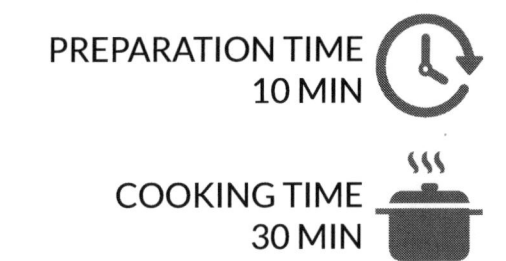

PREPARATION TIME 10 MIN

COOKING TIME 30 MIN

SERVINGS 2

INGREDIENTS:

- Cup turkey, cooked, cut into 1/2-inch cubes
- Cups vegetables, fresh or frozen or canned
- cups brown rice, cooked
- 1 Tablespoon oil
- 1/2 teaspoon sugar
- 1/2 Tablespoon ginger, minced
- 1/4 Teaspoon clove Garlic, minced
- 1/2 teaspoon salt

DIRECTIONS:

In a non-stick frying pan, heat oil at low-medium temperature.

Put the turkey, vegetables, minced ginger, garlic, and salt.

Stir and fry for about one minute.

Add sugar and continue stirring.

Reduce heat to avoid scorching and continue cooking until the vegetables become tender.

When the vegetables become tender, remove them from the heat.

In the event, if the vegetables did not cook well, pour 2-3 tablespoons of water and cook until it becomes soft.

Serve with the cooked rice.

Nutrition: Calories: 223 Total Fat: 12g Total Carbohydrates: 21g Fiber: 6g Sugar: 8g Protein: 13g

108. TUSCAN WHITE BEANS WITH SHRIMP, SPINACH, AND FETA

PREPARATION TIME 10 MIN
COOKING TIME 20 MIN
SERVINGS 2

INGREDIENTS:

- 1 Pound shrimp, large, peeled, and deveined
- 15 Ounces cannellini beans, saltless, rinsed and drained
- 1 1/2 Ounces low-fat feta cheese, shredded
- 1/2 cup chicken broth, fat-free, low-sodium
- 4 Cloves clove Garlic, minced
- 2 Teaspoons sage, fresh, finely chopped
- 2 Tablespoons balsamic vinegar
- 2 Tablespoons olive oil
- 1 medium-size onion, chopped
- 5 cups baby spinach

DIRECTIONS:

Take a large skillet

Pour one tablespoon of olive oil and bring to medium temperature.

When the oil becomes hot, put the shrimp for 2-3 minutes.

Transfer the shrimp to a plate when its color changes.

Pour the balance oil into the skillet and put chopped onion, sage, and garlic.

Stir and cook until the onion turns a golden color. Within 4 minutes of cooking, the onion will start to become a golden color.

Add vinegar and continue cooking for another half minute.

Now add the chicken broth and cook for two minutes until it boils.

At this time, add the vegetables and put the spinach. Cook until the spinach starts to wilt.

Get the skillet from the heat and put the cooked shrimp and stir.

Serve by topping with feta cheese.

Nutrition: Calories: 280 Total Fat: 7g Total Carbohydrates: 22g Fiber: 6g Sugar: 0.5g Protein: 32g

109. Chicken & Broccoli in Sesame Noodles

PREPARATION TIME
5 MIN

COOKING TIME
20 MIN

SERVINGS
2

INGREDIENTS:

- 1/2 Cup chicken, cooked & diced
- 8 Ounces whole-wheat spaghetti noodles
- 1/4 cup vegetable oil
- 12 Ounces broccoli florets, frozen
- Tablespoon garlic, minced
- Tablespoons sugar
- Tablespoons rice vinegar
- 2 Tablespoons soy sauce, low sodium
- 1 Tablespoon sesame seeds, toasted

DIRECTIONS:

Prepare pasta as per the package instructions and keep it aside.

In a medium bowl, whisk soy sauce, sugar, and vinegar and keep aside.

Add the oil in a skillet and bring to medium heat.

Put broccoli and garlic and cook until it becomes soft.

Now add the chicken pieces and cook very well for about 10 minutes.

When the chicken's color starts to change, add soy sauce mixture and pasta.

Mix it thoroughly.

Serve by drizzling sesame seeds on top.

Nutrition: Calories: 240 Total Fat: 9g Total Carbohydrates: 27g Fiber: 4g Sugar: 5g Protein: 13g

110. SPICY BAKED POTATOES

PREPARATION TIME
10 MIN

COOKING TIME
25 MIN

SERVINGS
2

INGREDIENTS:

- 4 medium-size sweet potatoes
- 1/3 cups black beans, canned, rinsed and drained
- 1/2 cup Greek yogurt no-fat
- 1 Teaspoon olive oil
- 1 Teaspoon taco seasoning, low sodium
- 1/2 cup red pepper, diced
- 1/2 cup onion, chopped
- 1/2 teaspoon paprika
- 1 teaspoon chili powder
- 1/2 Teaspoon cumin
- 1/2 cup Mexican cheese, low-fat
- 1/4 teaspoon salt
- 1/2 cup salsa

DIRECTIONS:

Make holes in the potato with a fork or any sharp kitchen tools.

Microwave it for about 8-10 minutes until it becomes tender.

In a bowl, mix taco seasoning with yogurt.

Now heat oil in a saucepan at medium temperature.

Put chopped onions, paprika, chili powder, peppers, cumin, and sauté continuously on medium heat until the onion gets caramelized.

Add salt and continue stirring. Wait for about 5 minutes to get the onion caramelized.

Now add the drained black beans; continue heating and stirring for about 5 minutes.

Using a fork, slice the potato lengthwise.

Serve it by dressing with 2 tablespoons of shredded cheese, 2 tablespoons of Greek yogurt mixture, black bean mixture 1/3, and 2 tablespoons of salsa.

Nutrition: Calories: 260 Total Fat: 15g Total Carbohydrates: 32g Fiber: 6g Sugar: 3g Protein: 5g

111. TANDOORI CHICKEN

PREPARATION TIME 10 MIN

COOKING TIME 20 MIN

SERVINGS 2

INGREDIENTS:

- 6 Pieces boneless chicken cut into 1-inch pieces
- 1 cup yogurt, plain, fatless
- 2 Tablespoons paprika
- 1 teaspoon yellow curry powder
- 1 teaspoon red pepper, crushed
- 1/2 cup lemon juice
- 5 cloves garlic cloves, minced
- 1 teaspoon ground ginger
- 6 Skewers, soaked in water for 15 minutes

DIRECTIONS:

Using a blender, combine yogurt, garlic, lemon juice, curry powder, red pepper, ginger, and paprika thoroughly until it becomes a smooth paste.

Set your over to 390°F and preheat.

On the soaked skewers, skew all chicken pieces.

Place the skewed chicken on a plain plate and marinate the chicken with the blended mix. Keep the remaining marinade mix for later use.

Cover the marinated skewed chicken and refrigerate for a better marinade effect.

Let it marinates for about 4 hours and after that, take it out and again brush with the remaining marinade mix.

Now, bake it for about 20 minutes or bake it until the chicken's secretion from the chicken stops or the meat gets pierced. Serve hot.

Nutrition: Calories: 112 Total Fat: 2g Total Carbohydrates: 11g Fiber: 2g Sugar: 1g Protein: 10g

112. PORK TENDERLOIN WITH SWEET POTATOES & APPLE

PREPARATION TIME 10 MIN

COOKING TIME 30 MIN

SERVINGS 2

INGREDIENTS:

- 12 Ounces of pork tenderloin
- 1 Potato, large, cut into 1/2" cubes
- 3/4 cup apple cider
- 1/4 cup apple cider vinegar
- 1/4 Teaspoon paprika, smoked
- 2 Tablespoons maple syrup
- 1/4 Teaspoon ginger, dried
- 1 Teaspoon ginger, fresh, minced
- 2 Tablespoons vegetable oil
- 1 Apple, cut into 1/2" cube size

DIRECTIONS:

Take a large bowl and start mixing smoked paprika, apple cider, maple syrup, apple cider vinegar, black pepper, ginger, and keep aside.

Set your oven to 360°F and preheat.

Take a large oven-safe sauté pan and heat oil at medium temperature.

Once the oil becomes hot, put the pork tenderloin. Continue cooking at medium temperature for about 10 minutes.

Flip sides and make sure to cook all sides evenly. Once the sides cooked well, remove them from the heat.

Arrange the sweet potatoes around the tenderloin. Pour apple cider mixture over it.

Cover the saucepan and bake it for about 10 minutes.

Place the sliced apple pieces around the pork tenderloin and bake for another 10 minutes, until the tenderloin temperature shows 340°F.

Once the temperature is reached at 340°F, stop baking and remove the pork tenderloin, potatoes and apple and allow it to settle for 10 minutes.

Heat the cider mixture and reduce to 1/4 cup.

Slice the pork to edible size. Serve along with sweet potatoes and apples.

Dress it with apple cider while serving.

Nutrition: Calories: 339 Total Fat: 12g Total Carbohydrates: 21g Fiber: 3g Sugar: 0g Protein: 35g

113. TASTY TORTILLA BAKE

PREPARATION TIME 15 MIN

COOKING TIME 30 MIN

SERVINGS 2

INGREDIENTS:

- 8 Tortilla, sliced into half
- 1 cup corn, frozen or fresh
- 1 Onion, green, chopped
- 3 Eggs
- 1 cup milk, fat-free
- 1 cup Monterey Jack cheese
- 1 cup black beans, cooked
- 2 Ounces green chilies, canned, chopped
- 1/2 teaspoon chili powder
- 1 Tomato, sliced
- 1/4 teaspoon salsa

DIRECTIONS:

Take an 8" square shaped baking tray and spray some cooking oil.

Set your oven to 370°F and preheat.

Layer in 5 tortilla halves in the bottom of the baking pan.

Top it with one-third of the cheese, beans, and corn layer by layer. Repeat the layering.

Beat egg in a bowl with chili powder, green chili, and milk. Now pour the mix over the tortilla.

Dress the tomato slice over the tortilla and spread the remaining cheese on top.

Bake it for 30 minutes and check to confirm its baking status.

Allow it to settle for another 10 minutes.

Serve with salsa.

Nutrition: Calories: 181 Total Fat: 8g Total Carbohydrates: 21g Fiber: 0g Sugar: 4g Protein: 4g

114. PEAR QUESADILLAS

PREPARATION TIME 10 MIN

COOKING TIME 15 MIN

SERVINGS 2

INGREDIENTS:

- 1 Cup pear, canned or fresh, cubed
- 1 cup cheddar cheese, grated
- 4 Medium size whole-wheat tortillas
- 1/2 cup green peppers, thinly chopped
- 2 Tablespoons Onion, finely chopped

DIRECTIONS:

Place two tortillas on a cutting board.

Drizzle 1/4 of the shredded cheese on both tortillas.

Equally divide the peppers, pears, and onion and place on both tortillas. Now place the remaining cheese on both tortillas.

Top the tortillas with the remaining two tortillas.

Take large non-stick sauté pan and bring to medium heat. Place the tortillas in the pan.

Cook for about 3-4 minutes until the bottoms side becomes slightly brown.

Using a spatula, flip the tortilla and cook the other side for 3-4 minutes.

Once it is ready, gently transfer to a serving plate and cook the second tortillas.

Follow the same previous Directions and cook until it is ready.

Before serving, cut the tortillas into 4 eatable sizes.

Serve hot, and you can refrigerate the balance for later consumption.

Nutrition: Calories: 217 Total Fat: 11g Total Carbohydrates: 19g Fiber: 2g Sugar: 5g Protein: 10g

115. Porcini Mushrooms with Pasta

PREPARATION TIME: 15 MIN

COOKING TIME: 20 MIN

SERVINGS: 2

INGREDIENTS:

- 1/4 Ounce porcini mushrooms, dried
- 1/2 Tablespoon onion, thinly chopped
- 3 Tablespoons tomatoes, sun-dried, drained, sliced
- 1/2 cup evaporated skim milk
- 1/8 Teaspoon pepper, white, grounded
- 1/2 Pound pasta
- 1 Green onion, cut into 1/4" diagonal shape
- 1 Tablespoon parmesan cheese, grated
- 1 Teaspoon butter, unsalted
- 1/8 Teaspoon salt

DIRECTIONS:

Wash mushrooms in running water. Put it in a hot water bowl for 10 minutes.

After that, drain and slice the mushrooms into 1/2" size.

Take a large non-stick sauté pan, put butter, and heat on medium temperature.

When the butter melted, add shallots and sauté for about one minute.

Now, add tomatoes and mushrooms and stir for about three minutes.

Pour milk, white pepper ground, salt, and bring to boil.

Wait for 15 minutes to simmer and let the volume reduce to a quarter.

Now cook the pasta in hot water. Once the pasta is cooked well, drain the water and shift the pasta to a serving bowl.

Transfer the sauce over the pasta and toss to mix it properly.

Drizzle the shredded parmesan cheese and scallions while serving.

Nutrition: Calories: 200 Total Fat: 2g Total Carbohydrates: 39g Fiber: 2g Sugar: 0g Protein: 8g

116. SHRIMP & NECTARINE SALAD

PREPARATION TIME 10 MIN

COOKING TIME 20 MIN

SERVINGS 2

INGREDIENTS:

- 1/3 cup orange juice
- 3 tablespoons cider vinegar
- 1-1/2 teaspoons Dijon mustard
- 1-1/2 teaspoons honey
- tablespoon minced fresh tarragon

Salad:
- 4 teaspoons canola oil, divided
- 1 cup fresh or frozen corn
- 1-pound shrimp, uncooked, peeled and deveined
- 1/2 teaspoon lemon-pepper seasoning
- 1/4 teaspoon salt
- 8 cups torn mixed salad greens
- medium nectarines, cut into 1-inch pieces
- 1 cup grape tomatoes, halved
- 1/2 cup finely chopped red onion

DIRECTIONS:

Mix orange juice, vinegar, mustard, and honey in a bowl until blended. Stir in tarragon.

With a medium skillet, heat 1 tsp oil over medium-high heat. Input your corn; keep cooking and stirring until 1-2 minutes or until crisp-soft. Keep away from the pan.

Spray shrimp with lemon, pepper, and salt. With the same skillet, heat leftover oil over medium-high heat. Put together shrimp; cook and stir 3-4 minutes or till you see shrimp turn pink. Stir in corn.

With a large pan, combine leftover ingredients. Drizzle with 1/3 cup dressing and toss to coat it.

Separate the mixture among four plates. Add with shrimp mixture; drizzle with leftover dressing. Serve warm.

Nutrition: Calories: 250 Total Fat: 7g Total Carbohydrates: 27g Fiber: 5g Sugar: 10g Protein: 23g

117. PORK CHOPS WITH TOMATO CURRY

PREPARATION TIME 15 MIN

COOKING TIME 25 MIN

SERVINGS 2

INGREDIENTS:

- 6 pork loin chops, boneless (6 oz. each)
- small onion
- 4 teaspoons butter (divided)
- medium apples, sliced thinly
- 1 can whole tomatoes, undrained
- teaspoons sugar
- 2 teaspoons curry powder
- 1/2 teaspoon salt
- 1/2 teaspoon chili powder
- cups hot cooked brown rice
- 2 tablespoons toasted slivered almonds, optional

DIRECTIONS:

Finely chopped the onion.

Prepare a stockpot, warm 2 teaspoons butter over medium-high heat. Brown pork chops in batches. Remove from pan.

Warm remaining butter in the same pan with over medium heat. Include onions; keep cooking and stirring 2-3 minutes or until softened.

Keep turning the apples, tomatoes, sugar, curry powder, salt, and chili powder. Gather to a boil, stirring consciously to break up tomatoes.

Return chops to pan. Reduce heat; simmer, uncovered, 5 minutes. Keep turning chops; cook it up to 3-5 minutes longer or until a thermometer inserted in pork are reads 145°.

Allow it cool for 5 minutes minimum before serving. Serve with rice and, if desired, sprinkle with almonds.

Nutrition: Calories: 143 Total Fat: 6g Total Carbohydrates: 9g Fiber: 2g Sugar: 6g Protein: 12g

118. THAI CHICKEN PASTA SKILLET

PREPARATION TIME 10 MIN
COOKING TIME 20 MIN
SERVINGS 2

INGREDIENTS:

- 6 ounces uncooked whole-wheat spaghetti
- 2 tsp. canola oil
- package fresh sugar snap peas, trimmed and cut diagonally into thin strips
- cups julienned carrots (about 8 ounces)
- cups shredded cooked chicken
- 1 cup Thai peanut sauce
- 1 medium cucumber, halved lengthwise, seeded, and sliced diagonally
- Chopped fresh cilantro, optional

DIRECTIONS:

Cook pasta consistent with package Directions:; drain.

Meanwhile, in a frying pan, warm oil over medium-high heat. Add snap peas and carrots; stir-fry 6-8 minutes or till crisp tender.

Add chicken, peanut sauce, and spaghetti; heat through, moving to mix.

Transfer to a serving plate. Add cucumber and, if desired, cilantro.

Nutrition: Calories: 400 Total Fat: 15g Total Carbohydrates: 40g Fiber: 6g Sugar: 10g Protein: 25g

119. CHILI-LIME GRILLED PINEAPPLE

PREPARATION TIME 5 MIN

COOKING TIME 10 MIN

SERVINGS 2

INGREDIENTS:
- fresh pineapple
- 2 tablespoons brown sugar
- 2 tablespoon lime juice
- 1 tablespoon olive oil
- 1 tablespoon honey or agave nectar
- 1-1/2 teaspoons chili powder
- Dash salt

DIRECTIONS:

Peel pineapple, removing any eyes from fruit.

Cut lengthwise into wedges; take away the core. In a very little bowl, combine the remaining ingredients till blended.

Brush pineapple with half the glaze; reserve the remaining mixture for basting.

Grill pineapple, for 2-4 minutes on each side or until lightly browned, occasionally basting with reserved glaze.

Nutrition: Calories: 97 Total Fat: 2g Total Carbohydrates: 20g Fiber: 1g Sugar: 17g Proteins: 1g

120. PEPPERED SOLE

PREPARATION TIME: 10 MIN
COOKING TIME: 15 MIN
SERVINGS: 2

INGREDIENTS:

- 2 tablespoons butter
- 2 cups sliced fresh mushrooms
- 2 garlic cloves, minced
- 4 sole fillets (4 ounces each)
- 1/4 teaspoon paprika
- 1/4 teaspoon lemon-pepper seasoning
- 1/8 teaspoon cayenne pepper
- medium tomato, chopped
- green onions, thinly sliced

DIRECTIONS:

Using a large skillet, heat butter over medium-high heat. Put mushrooms; cook and stir until softened.

Put garlic; cook 1 minute longer. Place fillets over mushrooms. Sprinkle with paprika, lemon pepper, and cayenne.

Cover and cook it over medium heat 5-10 minutes or until fish begins to flake easily with a fork.

Sprinkle with tomato and green onions.

Nutrition: Calories: 25 Total Fat: 16g Total Carbohydrates: 18g Fiber: 0g Sugar: 2g Protein: 10g

121. SHRIMP ORZO WITH FETA

PREPARATION TIME 10 MIN

COOKING TIME 15 MIN

SERVINGS 2

INGREDIENTS:
- 1-1/4 cups whole wheat orzo pasta (uncooked)
- 2 tbsp. olive oil
- 2 garlic cloves
- 2 medium tomatoes
- 2 tbsp. lemon juice
- 1-1/4 lb. uncooked shrimp (peeled and deveined)
- 2 tbsp. minced fresh cilantro
- 1/4 tsp. pepper
- 1/2 cup feta cheese (crumbled)

DIRECTIONS:

Chopped 2 medium tomatoes and 2 garlic cloves.

Cook orzo according to package Directions:. Better still, in a large pan, heat oil over a medium cooker.

Put garlic; cook and stir 1 minute. Include tomatoes and lemon juice. Then to a boil. Stir in shrimp.

Decrease the heat; simmer and uncover it until shrimp turn pink, 4-5 minutes.

Dry orzo, cilantro, and pepper to shrimp together; heat through.

Spray with feta cheese.

Nutrition: Calories: 340 Total Fat: 14g Total Carbohydrates: 33g Fiber: 4g Sugar: 2g Protein: 22g

122. BEEF AND BLUE CHEESE PENNE WITH PESTO

PREPARATION TIME 15 MIN

COOKING TIME 15 MIN

SERVINGS 2

INGREDIENTS:

- 2 cups uncooked whole wheat penne pasta
- 2 beef tenderloin steaks (6 ounces each)
- 1/4 teaspoon salt
- 1/4 teaspoon pepper
- 5 oz. fresh baby spinach (about 6 cups), coarsely chopped
- 2 cups grape tomatoes, halved
- 1/3 cup prepared pesto
- 1/4 cup chopped walnuts
- 1/4 cup crumbled Gorgonzola cheese

DIRECTIONS:

Cook pasta according to package Directions:.

.Meanwhile, sprinkle steaks with salt and pepper for under 5-7 minutes on each side or until meat reaches desired doneness. For medium thermometer should read 135°F; medium, 140°F; medium-well, 145°F).

Drain pasta; transfer to a large bowl. Add spinach, tomatoes, pesto, and walnuts; toss to coat.

Cut steak into thin slices. Serve pasta mixture with beef; sprinkle with cheese.

Nutrition: Calories: 530 Total Fat: 20g Total Carbohydrates: 49g Fiber: 9g Sugar: 0g Protein: 35g

123. CALIFORNIA QUINOA

PREPARATION TIME 10 MIN

COOKING TIME 20 MIN

SERVINGS 2

INGREDIENTS:

- 1 tablespoon olive oil
- 1 cup quinoa, rinsed and well-drained
- garlic cloves, minced
- 1 medium zucchini, chopped
- cups of water
- 3/4 cup garbanzo beans or chickpeas (canned)
- 1 medium tomato, finely chopped
- 1/2 cup crumbled feta cheese
- 1/4 cup finely chopped Greek olives
- 2 tablespoons minced fresh basil
- 1/4 teaspoon pepper

DIRECTIONS:

Rinsed and drained garbanzo beans or chickpeas.

With a large saucepan, heat oil across medium heat.

Include quinoa and garlic; stir and cook until 2-3 minutes or until quinoa is lightly colored.

Stir together in zucchini and water; bring to heat. Decrease to heat; simmer, covered, till liquid is dry, 12-15 minutes.

Stir in the leftover ingredients; heat thoroughly.

Nutrition: Calories: 160 Total Fat: 7g Total Carbohydrates: 20g Fiber: 4g Sugar: 10g Protein: 4g

124. PEPPERED TUNA KABOBS

PREPARATION TIME 10 MIN

COOKING TIME 20 MIN

SERVINGS 2

INGREDIENTS:

- 1/2 cup frozen corn, thawed
- 4 green onions
- jalapeno pepper, seeded
- tablespoons fresh parsley
- tbsp. lime juice
- 1 lb. tuna steaks, cut into 1-inch cubes
- 1 tsp. coarsely ground pepper
- 1 medium mango, peeled
- 2 large sweet red peppers

DIRECTIONS:

Chopped green onions, fresh parsley and jalapeno pepper.

Cut mango into 1-inch cubes and red peppers into 2x1 inch.

Add salsa, in a little bowl, add the first five ingredients; set aside.

Rub tuna with pepper. Use four metal or soaked wooden skewers or thread red peppers, tuna, and mango.

Use skewers on a greased grill rack. Cover it and cook over medium heat, keep always turning, until tuna is slightly turned to pink in center (medium-rare) and peppers are soft, 10-12 minutes.

Good with salsa.

Nutrition: Calories: 205 Total Fat: 2g Total Carbohydrates: 20g Fiber: 4g Sugar: 12g Protein: 29g

SNACK

125. MINI BELL PEPPER LOADED NACHOS

PREPARATION TIME 10 MIN

COOKING TIME 20 MIN

SERVINGS 2

INGREDIENTS:

- Olive oil spray
- lb. 93% lean ground turkey or beef
- 1 clove garlic, minced
- 1/4 onion, minced
- 1 Tbsp. chopped fresh cilantro or parsley
- 1 tsp. garlic powder
- 1 tsp. cumin powder
- 1 tsp. chili powder
- 1 tsp. onion powder
- 1/4 tsp. kosher salt
- 1/4 cup tomato sauce
- 1/4 cup chicken broth
- 21 mini sweet peppers, halved and seeded
- 1 cup low-fat sharp Cheddar cheese, shredded
- 1 Tbsp. Light sour cream, thinned with 1 Tbsp. water
- 1 Tbsp. sliced black olives
- Optional:
- 1 jalapeno, sliced thin
- Chopped cilantro, for garnish
- 1/2 tsp. crushed red pepper flakes

DIRECTIONS:

Preheat oven to 400 degrees F

Prepare baking tray with parchment or aluminum foil, lightly spray with oil.

Put oil in a nonstick skillet over medium heat.

Add onion, garlic, and cilantro. Sauté for about 2 minutes.

Add the ground turkey, salt, garlic powder, cumin and cook meat for 4 to 5 minutes until meat is completely cooked through.

Put the tomato sauce and chicken broth, mix well. Let it simmer on medium heat for about 5 minutes, remove from heat.

In the meantime, arrange mini peppers in a single layer, cut side up and close together.

Fill each one with the cooked ground turkey mixture, then top with the shredded cheese and jalapeno slices, if desired.

Bake until cheese is melted or about 8 minutes. Remove from the oven and top with black olives, sour cream and cilantro. Serve!

Nutrition: Calories: 228 Total Fat: 13g Total Carbohydrates: 11g Fiber: 3g Sugar: 4g Protein: 18g

PREPARATION TIME
15 MIN

COOKING TIME
15 MIN

SERVINGS
2

126. ZUCCHINI PIZZA BOATS

INGREDIENTS:

- 2-3 small zucchini
- 1 Tbsp. olive oil
- 1 clove garlic, finely minced
- Freshly ground black pepper
- 1 cup marinara sauce, no sugar
- 1/2 cup reduced-fat mozzarella cheese, shredded
- 1 Tbsp. Parmesan cheese, finely shredded
- Italian seasoning blend, no salt
- 1 tbsp. chopped fresh oregano
- 1/4 tsp. salt

Optional toppings:
- Sautéed onion
- Sun-dried tomatoes
- Mushrooms, chopped
- Crushed red pepper flakes

DIRECTIONS:

Preheat oven to 400 degrees F.

Get a rimmed baking sheet with parchment paper. Set aside.

Slice zucchini into halves through the length, making sure they lie flat by trimming a thin portion on the bottom

Then pat the inside of the zucchinis dry with a paper towel and place them on the prepared baking sheet, set aside.

Get a bowl then mix olive oil and garlic in a bowl then brush it lightly over zucchini tops.

Sprinkle with the Italian seasoning and pepper to taste

Slightly brush one tablespoon marinara sauce over each zucchini, leaving a small rim near edges uncoated.

Sprinkle the tops evenly with mozzarella cheese, then with parmesan cheese.

Top with the sautéed onions, sun-dried tomatoes, chopped mushrooms and crushed red pepper flakes, if desired

Cook for 15 minutes, or until how crisp you want them.

Remove from oven and sprinkle with fresh oregano and serve!

Nutrition: Calories: 214 Total Fat: 8g Total Carbohydrates: 24g Fiber: 4g Sugar: 5g Protein: 15g

127. FRUIT SKEWERS WITH VANILLA HONEY YOGURT DIP

PREPARATION TIME 10 MIN

COOKING TIME 10 MIN

SERVINGS 2

INGREDIENTS:

Fruit Skewers:
- 10 strawberries
- 20 blueberries
- pineapple, cored and cubed
- kiwis, peeled and cubed
- 10 bamboo skewers
- Vanilla Yogurt Dip:
- 1/2 cups non-fat Greek yogurt
- 8 oz. non-fat or low-fat cream cheese
- 1/4 cup honey
- 1 tsp. vanilla extract

DIRECTIONS:

Cut up the pineapple and kiwis into even squares.

Take the blueberries, strawberries, kiwis and pineapple squares and place them onto the skewers in a rainbow color order.

Then create the yogurt dip, combine yogurt, cream cheese, honey and vanilla extract in a bowl. Mix well until combined.

Plate the fruits on a serving dish and serve with the vanilla yogurt dip.

Nutrition: Calories: 215 Total Fat: 3g Total Carbohydrates: 50g Fiber: 5g Sugar: 30g Protein: 4g

128. BAKED PARMESAN ZUCCHINI STICKS

PREPARATION TIME 10 MIN

COOKING TIME 20 MIN

SERVINGS 2

INGREDIENTS:

- 3 medium zucchinis, sliced into sticks
- 1 cup whole wheat breadcrumbs
- 1/2 cup Parmesan cheese, grated
- 1 egg
- 1/4 tsp. salt
- 1/4 tsp. pepper or to taste

Optional:
- Ranch dressing, for dipping
- Low-sodium Marinara sauce, for dipping

DIRECTIONS:

Preheat oven to 425 degrees F.

Get baking sheet with parchment paper, set aside Slice the zucchinis in to sticks.

In a bowl, beat the eggs, season with salt and pepper.

In a different bowl, combine the Panko breadcrumbs with the Parmesan cheese, season with salt and pepper

Soak each zucchini stick into the egg wash and roll it in the breadcrumb mixture.

Arrange on the baking sheet then bake until crispy and golden brown.

Serve with Ranch dressing or Marinara sauce.

Nutrition: Calories: 128 Total Fat: 7g Total Carbohydrates: 10g Fiber: 1g Sugar: 1g Protein: 6g

129. SPINACH ARTICHOKE DIP

PREPARATION TIME 5 MIN

COOKING TIME 30 MIN

SERVINGS 2

INGREDIENTS:

- 2 cups artichoke hearts
- 4 cups spinach, chopped
- cup white beans, cooked
- 1/2 cup low-fat sour cream
- Tbsp. Parmesan cheese
- Tbsp. black pepper
- 1 tsp. thyme, minced
- cloves garlic, minced
- Tbsp. parsley, minced

DIRECTIONS:

Preheat the oven to 350 degrees F.

Put artichoke hearts, spinach, cream cheese, sour cream, white beans, black pepper, thyme, garlic and parsley in a large bowl. Stir well to combine.

Put the mixture to a glass or ceramic dish

Bake for 30 minutes.

Serve with whole-grain bread, crackers or vegetables for dipping.

Nutrition: Calories: 100 Total Fat: 8g Total Carbohydrates: 3g Fiber: 1g Sugar: 1g Protein: 3g

130. BUFFALO CHICKPEA AND ARTICHOKE TAQUITOS

PREPARATION TIME 15 MIN

COOKING TIME 15 MIN

SERVINGS 2

INGREDIENTS:

- 2 can chickpeas (clean and drained) or 3 cups cooked chickpeas
- cup low sodium chopped artichoke hearts, frozen or canned, drained
- 1 cup fat-reduced cheese sauce
- 1/4 - 1/2 cup Buffalo style hot sauce
- 15-20 small tortillas, corn or flour

Dipping Sauce, optional:
- Guacamole

DIRECTIONS:

Ready your oven to 425 degrees F.

Mash the chickpeas in a bowl.

Add the chopped artichoke hearts, cheese sauce and buffalo style hot sauce, mix to combine.

Get about 2 tbsp. of the filling onto each tortilla and roll tightly.

Place them seam side down onto a baking sheet.

Bake 15 to 20 minutes until the tortillas are browning on the edges

Serve hot!

Nutrition: Calories: 154 Total Fat: 6g Total Carbohydrates: 22g Fiber: 4g Sugar: 2g Protein: 4g

131. LOADED AVOCADO QUESADILLAS

PREPARATION TIME 15 MIN

COOKING TIME 30 MIN

SERVINGS 2

INGREDIENTS:

For Filling:
- 2 Tbsp. olive oil
- 2 tsp. ground cumin
- 3 tbsp. lime juice
- 1/2 tsp. chipotle chile powder
- 1/4 tsp. black pepper
- 3 minced garlic cloves
- tsp. maple syrup or agave
- 1 red bell pepper, sliced into strips
- 1 medium zucchini, chopped
- 1/2 medium red onion
- 1 jalapeño pepper
- 1 cup cooked or canned black beans (wash and drain if using canned)
- 1/4 cup chopped fresh cilantro
- 1/4 tsp. salt

For the Quesadillas:
- 4 to 6 medium flour tortillas
- 2 Avocados (ripe)
- Oil, for grilling

DIRECTIONS:

Slice jalapeno pepper and remove seed. Cut the red onion into strips.

Put lime juice, olive oil, cumin, chipotle chili powder, salt, pepper, garlic and agave or maple syrup in a bowl, mix well. Add the bell pepper, zucchini, onion and jalapeño to the bowl and toss to coat.

Place a large skillet over medium-high heat. Add and cook veggies, flipping frequently, until most of the liquid has cooked off and veggies are tender-crisp, about 4 minutes.

Remove from heat and add the beans and cilantro, flipping a few times to incorporate, then transfer the mixture to a plate.

Get a small bowl and gently mash the avocados with a fork. Put mashed avocado onto half of a tortilla, sprinkle with salt and pepper, and optionally with some hot sauce.

Put even layer of veggies over avocado, fold the tortilla closed over the veggies, and repeat until all the filling is used.

Warm oil in a heated skillet. Arrange one or two tortillas onto skillet and grill until browned and crispy on the bottom, about 4 minutes.

Turn and grill opposite side, about 4 minutes more, repeat until all quesadillas are cooked, adding oil to the skillet as needed.

Serve with hot sauce or salsa.

Nutrition: Calories: 290 Total Fat: 18g Total Carbohydrates: 32g Fiber: 10g Sugar: 1g Protein: 7g

132. CRUNCHY KALE CHIPS

PREPARATION TIME
5 MIN

COOKING TIME
10 MIN

SERVINGS
2

INGREDIENTS:

- 12 (or more) flat-leaf kale leaves
- Oil spray
- Zesty no-salt seasoning of your choice, such as garlic powder or Cajun seasoning

Optional:
- Ground Pepper, to taste

DIRECTIONS:

Preheat oven to 400 degrees F.

Using scissors, cut 12 (or more) kale leaves into the size of a large potato chip.

Lay the kale onto a large nonstick baking sheet or sheets, do not overlap.

Lightly mist them with oil spray, then season with freshly ground black pepper or the zesty no-salt-added seasoning of your choice

Cook in oven for 10 minutes. Remove from the oven

Enjoy!

Nutrition: Calories: 90 Total Fat: 6g Total Carbohydrates: 6g Fiber: 2g Sugar: 1g Protein: 4g

133. CRISPY PARMESAN RANCH ZUCCHINI CHIPS

PREPARATION TIME 10 MIN

COOKING TIME 30 MIN

SERVINGS 2

INGREDIENTS:

- 3 Medium zucchini squash, washed, ends trimmed off
- Large egg white
- 1/4 cup Parmesan cheese, grated
- tsp. dried parsley flakes
- 1 1/2 tsp. dill weed seasoning
- 1 tsp. garlic powder
- 1 tsp. onion powder
- 1/4 tsp. salt
- 1/4 tsp. pepper

DIRECTIONS:

Preheat oven to 425 degrees F.

Get a baking sheet pan with foil and spray with cooking spray, set aside.

Cut the zucchini into 1/8-inch disks, try to cut the disks the same thickness to make sure they cook evenly.

In a large zip lock bag, add the parmesan, dried parsley flakes, dill weed seasoning, garlic powder, onion, salt and pepper, shake to combine, set aside.

Add egg white in a bowl and whisk until frothy.

Place the zucchini slices in the bowl with the egg whites, and toss the zucchini the in-egg white, until they are coated evenly.

Then place the zucchini slices in Ziplock bag with Parmesan seasoning and shake to coat zucchini with coating.

Place the zucchini chips on prepared baking pan. Bake for 25 minutes.

Once cooked, turn on the ovens broilers, and broil under high heat for about 1-2 minutes, or just until coating is lightly browned and crispy on the outside.

Remove from the oven and serve warm with dipping sauce of choice!

Nutrition: Calories: 110 Total Fat: 4g Total Carbohydrates: 11g Fiber: 3g Sugar: 6g Protein: 9g

134. CINNAMON YOGURT FRUIT DIP

PREPARATION TIME
5 MIN

COOKING TIME
5 MIN

SERVINGS
2

INGREDIENTS:

- Yogurt, plain, low-fat – 1 cup
- Cinnamon, ground - 1/2 teaspoon
- Honey – 2 tablespoons
- Vanilla extract - 1/4 teaspoon

DIRECTIONS:

Whisk together all of the ingredients.

Taste and adjust the cinnamon, vanilla, or honey to your preference.

Serve the dip immediately or store it in the fridge for up to five days before serving.

Nutrition: Calories: 103 Total Fat: 1g Total Carbohydrates: 18g Fiber: 0g Sugar: 2g Protein: 5g

135. CHOCOLATE YOGURT PUDDING

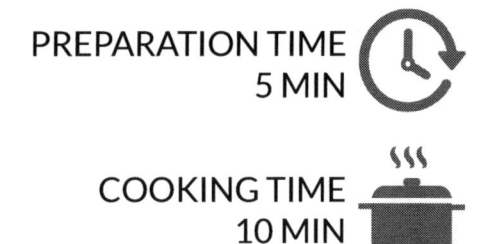

PREPARATION TIME
5 MIN

COOKING TIME
10 MIN

SERVINGS
2

INGREDIENTS:

- Greek yogurt, plain, fat-free – 1/2 cup
- Maple syrup – 1 1/2 tablespoons
- Dark cocoa powder – 2 tablespoons

DIRECTIONS:

Whisk together everything in a bowl until all the lumps have dissolved.

If your pudding is too thick, then feel free to add a couple teaspoons of skim milk, as each brand of yogurt has its unique thickness.

Adjust the sweetness to taste by adjusting the maple syrup level to your preference.

Nutrition: Calories: 140 Total Fat: 3g Total Carbohydrates: 20g Fiber: 2g Sugar: 6g Protein: 11g

136. PEANUT BUTTER ENERGY BITES

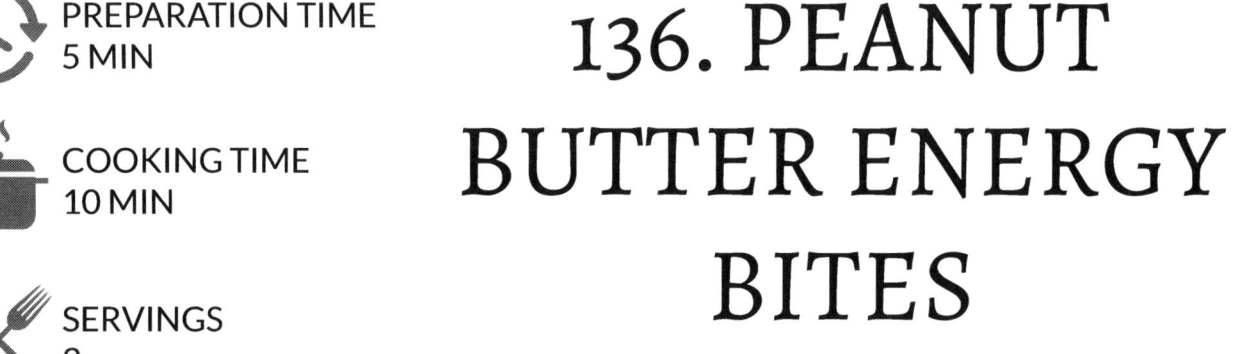

PREPARATION TIME
5 MIN

COOKING TIME
10 MIN

SERVINGS
2

INGREDIENTS:

- Peanut butter, low-sodium – 2/3 cup
- Rolled oats – 1 cup
- Semi-sweet chocolate chips – 1/2 cup
- Flaxseeds, ground – 1/2 cup
- Honey – 2 tablespoons

DIRECTIONS:

Get a medium bowl and use a spatula to mix all the ingredients until evenly combined.

Put cover and place it in the fridge to set up for fifteen to thirty minutes, making them easy to handle and roll.

Divide the dough into twelve evenly sized portions and then roll each portion into a ball.

Put into an airtight container and store them in the fridge.

Nutrition: Calories: 100 Total Fat: 6g Total Carbohydrates: 11g Fiber: 0g Sugar: 7g Proteins: 3g

137. APPLE PIE OAT BARS

PREPARATION TIME 5 MIN

COOKING TIME 25 MIN

SERVINGS 26

INGREDIENTS:

- Rolled oats – 1 cup
- Quick cooking oats – 1 cup
- Cinnamon, ground – 1 1/2 teaspoons
- Chia seeds – 2 tablespoons
- Light olive oil – 2 tablespoons
- Applesauce, unsweetened – 1 cup
- Honey – 2 tablespoons

DIRECTIONS:

Warm the oven to Fahrenheit 375 degrees and line a nine-by-nine-inch baking dish with kitchen parchment.

Mix the oats, cinnamon, and chia seeds in a small bowl. Once combined, add in the oil, applesauce, and honey.

Arrange the dough into the bottom of the baking dish in an even layer. Put the pan in the oven to cook until set but still soft, about 25 minutes.

Remove the dish from the oven and allow it to cool for a few minutes before slicing and serving.

Nutrition: Calories: 170 Total Fat: 6g Total Carbohydrates: 30g Fiber: 2g Sugar: 9g Protein: 3g

138. BAKED CHICKEN NUGGETS

PREPARATION TIME 10 MIN

COOKING TIME 15 MIN

SERVINGS 2

INGREDIENTS:

- Chicken breast, boneless and skinless – 1 pound
- Eggs – 2
- Whole-wheat flour - .75 cup
- Breadcrumbs, low-sodium – 2 cups
- Garlic powder – 1/2 teaspoon
- Black pepper, ground – 1/2 teaspoon
- Dijon mustard – 1 tablespoon

DIRECTIONS:

Warm the oven to Fahrenheit 375 degrees. Place a wire cooling/cooking rack on a baking sheet, spray it with non-stick cooking spray, and then set it aside.

Slice the chicken breast into bite-sized cubes, about 1-inch each. Try to cut these cubes as evenly in size as possible, so that the chicken cooks evenly.

Setup a breading station to coat your chicken nuggets. To do this, keep the chicken cubes on a large plate, the flour in one bowl, the egg and mustard beaten together in another bowl, and the breadcrumbs in yet another bowl.

Sprinkle the black pepper over the chicken and add the garlic powder to the flour, stirring it in until combined.

One at a time, coat the chicken cubes in first the flour, followed by the egg, and lastly the breadcrumbs.

Place the chicken cubes on the wire rack that is placed on the baking sheet. Repeat this process until all of your chicken nuggets are coated.

Place the nuggets in the oven to cook completely until they are crispy with an inside temperature of Fahrenheit 165 degrees with a meat thermometer—about 15 minutes.

Serve the nuggets hot and enjoy.

Nutrition: Calories: 120 Total Fat: 3g Total Carbohydrates: 10g Fiber: 1g Sugar: 1g Protein: 11g

139. CINNAMON APPLES

PREPARATION TIME
5 MIN

COOKING TIME
10 MIN

SERVINGS
22

INGREDIENTS:

- Apples – 4 pounds
- Light olive oil – 2 tablespoons
- Honey – 1/4 cup
- Apple juice – 1/4 cup
- Allspice, ground – 1/2 teaspoon
- Cinnamon, ground – 2 teaspoons
- Cornstarch – 2 teaspoons
- Apple cider vinegar – 1 teaspoon

DIRECTIONS:

Peel the apples and core them before slicing them. Slice each apple into eight wedges so that they are all the same thickness.

Add all of the ingredients—except for the apple cider vinegar—into a large skillet or Dutch oven and mix carefully to distribute the spices and cornstarch.

Cover the pan with a lid and allow the apples to simmer over medium-low heat for eight minutes or until tender.

Get the apples from the heat and stir in the apple cider vinegar. Serve the apples warm or cold.

Store any leftovers in the fridge for up to a week or in the freezer for several months.

Nutrition: Calories: 130 Total Fat: 2g Total Carbohydrates: 26g Fiber: 1g Sugar: 10g Protein: 0g

140. RANCH AND CHEESE BELL PEPPER POPPERS

PREPARATION TIME 10 MIN

COOKING TIME 30 MIN

SERVINGS 2

INGREDIENTS:

- Mini bell peppers – 1 pound
- Cheddar cheese, low-fat, shredded – 1 cup
- Cream cheese, low-fat, room temperature – 8 ounces
- Mayonnaise, low-fat – .33 cup
- Garlic powder – 1/2 teaspoon
- Onion powder - 1/2 teaspoon
- Chives, dried – 1/2 teaspoon
- Parsley, dried - 1/2 teaspoon
- Black pepper, ground - 1/4 teaspoon

DIRECTIONS:

Cut bell pepper in half and seeded.

Mix the cream cheese, cheddar cheese, mayonnaise, and seasonings until fully combined.

With a spoon scoop out small portions of the cream cheese mixture and stuff it into the mini bell pepper halves.

Place the stuffed bell peppers in the fridge to chill for at least thirty minutes before serving.

Enjoy cold.

Nutrition: Calories: 130 Total Fat: 5g Total Carbohydrates: 20g Fiber: 1g Sugar: 1g Protein: 2g

141. BAKED CHICKEN TACOS

PREPARATION TIME 5 MIN

COOKING TIME 15-20 MIN

SERVINGS 2

INGREDIENTS:

- Corn tortillas, low-sodium – 6
- Chicken breast, cooked, chopped – 6 ounces
- Cheddar cheese, low-fat – 1/2 cup

DIRECTIONS:

Warm the oven to Fahrenheit 400 degrees and prepare two large baking sheets.

Wet a couple of paper or kitchen towels with water and wrap them around the corn tortillas, setting them on a dinner plate.

Microwave the wrapped tortillas for thirty seconds, flip them over, and then microwave for thirty more seconds.

Place the warm corn tortillas on the prepared baking sheet. On one half of each tortilla, sprinkle the cheese and chicken breast.

Fold over one half of the tortilla over the filing, so that you are left with a taco shape. After all of your tacos are folding in half, take the second baking pan and place it on top of the tacos to hold them all in place so that they can't open.

Place the tacos in the oven and allow them to bake until they turn golden-brown, about eight to twelve minutes. Watch the tacos carefully as they can burn quickly. If you want your tacos extra crispy, you can remove the top baking sheet the last few minutes of cooking, after the cheese has melted and holds the tacos in place and sealed.

Serve the tacos hot alone or with your favorite low-sodium toppings, such as homemade salsa, guacamole, salsa Verde, our light sour cream.

Nutrition: Calories: 159 Total Fat: 6g Total Carbohydrates: 10g Fiber: 1g Sugar: 0.4g Protein: 16g

142. SWEET AND SPICY ROASTED SWEET POTATO ROUNDS

PREPARATION TIME 10 MIN

COOKING TIME 30 MIN

SERVINGS 2

INGREDIENTS:

- Sweet potatoes – 2
- Extra virgin olive oil – 3 tablespoons
- Chili powder – 1 teaspoon
- Garlic powder – 1/2 teaspoon
- Onion powder – 1/2 teaspoon
- Cumin, ground – 1/2 teaspoon
- Chili flakes – 1/4 teaspoon
- Honey – 1 tablespoon

DIRECTIONS:

Warm the oven to Fahrenheit 425 degrees and like a large baking sheet with kitchen parchment.

Wash the sweet potatoes, leaving the peel on. Slice them into rounds each 1/2-inch thick.

Into a bowl toss the sweet potatoes with the olive oil and spices until fully and evenly coated.

Arrange the sweet potato rounds into a single layer on the baking sheet and place them in the oven about twenty-five minutes until tender all the way through and caramelized. Halfway through the cooking time flip the rounds over so that they can cook evenly.

Take out the sweet potatoes from the oven and drizzle the honey over the top before serving.

You can also add a hint of lime juice for an extra punch of flavor, if you want.

Nutrition: Calories: 158 Total Fat: 5g Total Carbohydrates: 27g Fiber: 3g Sugar: 0g Protein: 2g

DESSERT

143. EASY BROWNIES

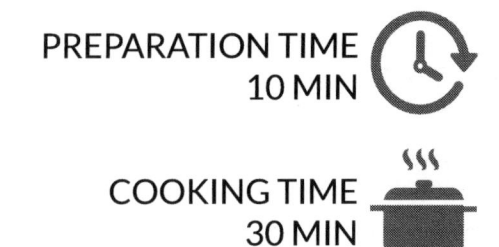

PREPARATION TIME
10 MIN

COOKING TIME
30 MIN

SERVINGS
2

INGREDIENTS:

- 6 ounces dark chocolate, chopped
- 4 egg whites
- 1/2 cup hot water
- 1 teaspoon vanilla extract
- 2/3 cup coconut sugar
- 1 and 1/2 cups whole flour
- 1/2 cup walnuts, chopped
- Cooking spray
- 1 teaspoon baking powder

DIRECTIONS:

In a bowl, combine the chocolate and the hot water and whisk well.

Add vanilla extract and egg whites and whisk well again.

In another bowl, combine the sugar with flour, baking powder, and walnuts and stir.

Combine the 2 mixtures, stir well, pour this into a cake pan greased with cooking spray, spread well, bake in the oven for 30 minutes, cool down, slice, and serve.

Enjoy!

Nutrition: Calories: 140 Total Fat: 10g Total Carbohydrates: 14g Fiber: 1g Sugar: 8g Protein: 2g

144. VANILLA BLACK BEAN BROWNIES

PREPARATION TIME 10 MIN

COOKING TIME 20 MIN

SERVINGS 22

INGREDIENTS:

- 1/2 cups canned black beans, no-salt-added, drained and rinsed
- 2 tablespoons coconut sugar
- 1/2 cup quick oats
- 2 tablespoons cocoa powder
- 1/3 cup maple syrup
- 1/4 cup coconut oil, melted
- 1/2 teaspoon baking powder
- 2 teaspoons vanilla extract
- Cooking spray

DIRECTIONS:

Prepare the oven at 350 degrees F.

In your food processor, combine the black beans with coconut sugar, oats, cocoa powder, maple syrup, oil, baking powder and vanilla extract and pulse well.

Grease a square pan with cooking spray, add the black beans mix, spread.

Cook for 20 minutes, leave aside to cool down, slice and serve.

Enjoy!

Nutrition: Calories: 144 Total Fat: 7g Total Carbohydrates: 18g Fiber: 2g Sugar: 10g Proteins: 3g

145. APPLE TART

PREPARATION TIME
10 MIN

COOKING TIME
25 MIN

SERVINGS
2

INGREDIENTS:

- 4 apples, cored, peeled, and sliced
- 1/4 cup natural apple juice
- 1/2 cup cranberries, dried
- 2 tablespoons cornstarch
- 2 teaspoons coconut sugar
- 1 teaspoon vanilla extract
- 1/4 teaspoon cinnamon powder

For the crust:
- 1/4 cup whole wheat flour
- 2 teaspoons sugar
- 3 tablespoons coconut oil, melted
- 1/4 cup cold water

DIRECTIONS:

In a bowl, combine the cranberries with the apple juice.

In another bowl, combine the apples with cornstarch, toss and add the cranberries mix.

Stir everything, add vanilla and cinnamon and stir everything again.

In a separate bowl, mix the flour with the sugar, oil and cold water and stir until you obtain a dough.

Transfer the dough to a working surface, flatten well, roll into a circle and transfer to a tart pan.

Press the crust well into the pan, add the apples mix over the crust, bake for 25 minutes at 375 degrees F, cool it down, slice and serve.

Enjoy!

Nutrition: Calories: 160 Total Fat: 8g Total Carbohydrates: 17g Fiber: 1g Sugar: 7g Protein: 2g

146. CHOCOLATE CAKE

PREPARATION TIME
10 MIN

COOKING TIME
25 MIN

SERVINGS
20

INGREDIENTS:

- 3 cups whole wheat flour
- 1 cup coconut sugar
- 1 tablespoon vanilla extract
- 3 tablespoons cocoa powder
- 2 tablespoons vinegar
- 2 and 1/2 teaspoons baking soda
- 2 cups hot water
- 1/2 cup coconut oil, melted

DIRECTIONS:

In a bowl, combine the flour with the baking soda, sugar, flour and cocoa powder and stir.

Put this into a baking pan, make 3 holes in this mix, add the vanilla extract in one, the oil in another and the vinegar in the third one.

Add the water over the mix from the pan, whisk everything for 2 minutes, introduce in the oven at 350 degrees F, bake for 25 minutes, leave the cake to cool down, slice and serve.

Enjoy!

Nutrition: Calories: 249 Total Fat: 13g Total Carbohydrates: 34g Fiber: 1g Sugar: 1g Protein: 2g

147. BANANA CAKE

PREPARATION TIME 10 MIN

COOKING TIME 25 MIN

SERVINGS 2

INGREDIENTS:

- 2 cups whole wheat flour
- 1/4 cup cocoa powder
- 1 banana, peeled and mashed
- 1/2 teaspoon baking soda
- 1/2 cup coconut sugar
- 3/4 cup almond milk
- 1/4 cup coconut oil, melted
- 1 egg
- 1 egg white
- 1 teaspoon vanilla extract
- 1 tablespoon lemon juice
- Cooking spray

DIRECTIONS:

In a bowl, combine the flour with the cocoa powder, baking soda and sugar and stir.

Add banana, milk, oil, egg, egg white, vanilla and lemon juice and stir well.

Grease a cake pans with cooking spray, pour the cake mix spread.

Bake in the oven at 350 degrees F for 25 minutes, cool down, slice and serve.

Enjoy!

Nutrition: Calories: 270 Total Fat: 14g Total Carbohydrates: 36g Fiber: 0.5g Sugar: 20g Protein: 2g

148. APPLE CUPCAKES

PREPARATION TIME
10 MIN

COOKING TIME
22 MIN

SERVINGS
22

INGREDIENTS:

- 4 tablespoons coconut butter
- 1/2 cup natural applesauce
- 4 eggs
- 1 teaspoon vanilla extract
- 3/4 cup almond flour
- 2 teaspoons cinnamon powder
- 1/2 teaspoon baking powder
- 1 apple, cored and sliced

DIRECTIONS:

Dissolve butter in a pan with medium heat.

Add applesauce, vanilla and eggs, stir, heat up for 2 minutes.

Take off heat, cool down, add almond flour, baking powder and cinnamon, stir.

Divide into a lined cupcake pan, introduce in the oven at 350 degrees F and bake for 20 minutes.

Leave the cupcakes to cool down, divide between dessert plates and top with apple slices.

Nutrition: Calories: 163 Total Fat: 8g Total Carbohydrates: 22g Fiber: 1g Sugar: 1g Protein: 2g

149. EASY FUDGE

PREPARATION TIME
15 MIN

COOKING TIME
30 MIN

SERVINGS
22

INGREDIENTS:

- 1/2 cup low-fat butter
- 12 ounces dark chocolate, chopped
- 1 teaspoon vanilla extract
- 2 cups coconut sugar
- 1 cup non-fat milk

DIRECTIONS:

Heat up a pan with the milk over medium heat, add the sugar and the butter, stir and cook everything for 7 minutes.

Take this off heat, add the chocolate and whisk everything.

Pour this into a lined square pan, spread well, keep in the fridge for 30 minutes or more, cut into small squares and serve.

Enjoy!

Nutrition: Calories: 150 Total Fat: 2g Total Carbohydrates: 28g Fiber: 1g Sugar: 20g Protein: 6g

PREPARATION TIME
10 MIN

COOKING TIME
5 MIN

SERVINGS
2

150. FRUIT SALAD

INGREDIENTS:
- 1 teaspoon vanilla extract
- 1 watermelon, peeled and chopped
- 1 cup strawberries, chopped
- 1 cup kiwis, peeled and chopped
- 1 cup blueberries
- 1 teaspoon coconut sugar
- 8 ounces non-fat yogurt
- 8 ounces low-fat cream cheese

DIRECTIONS:
In a bowl, combine the watermelon with the vanilla, strawberries, kiwis, blueberries, sugar, yogurt and cream cheese, toss.

Divide into small cups and serve cold.

Nutrition: Calories: 110 Total Fat: 0g Total Carbohydrates: 17g Fiber: 0g Sugar: 0g Protein: 2g

151. RHUBARB PIE

PREPARATION TIME 10 MIN

COOKING TIME 30 MIN

SERVINGS 22

INGREDIENTS:

- 2 cups whole wheat flour
- 1 cup pecans, chopped
- 1 cup low-fat butter, melted
- 1 and 1/4 cup coconut sugar
- 4 cups rhubarb, chopped
- 1 cup strawberries, sliced
- 8 ounces low-fat cream cheese

DIRECTIONS:

In a bowl, combine the flour with the butter, pecans and 1/4 cup sugar and stir well.

Ready the oven at 350 degrees F.

Transfer this to a pie pan, press well.

Move pan in the oven and bake for 20 minutes.

In a pan, combine the strawberries with the rhubarb, cream cheese and 1 cup sugar, stir well and cook over medium heat for 4 minutes.

Spread this over the pie crust and keep in the fridge for a few hours before slicing and serving.

Nutrition: Calories: 280 Total Fat: 11g Total Carbohydrates: 35g Fiber: 3g Sugar: 10g Protein: 2g

152. BLUEBERRY CURD

PREPARATION TIME
10 MIN

COOKING TIME
10 MIN

SERVINGS
2

INGREDIENTS:
- 2 tablespoons lemon juice
- 2 tablespoons coconut oil, melted
- 3 tablespoons coconut sugar
- 12 ounces blueberries
- 2 eggs

DIRECTIONS:
Put the oil in a pot, heat up over medium heat, add lemon juice and coconut sugar and whisk well.

Add the blueberries and the eggs, whisk well, cook for 10 minutes.

Divide into small cups and serve cold.

Nutrition: Calories: 200 Total Fat: 13g Total Carbohydrates: 15g Fiber: 0g Sugar: 0g Protein: 6g

153. COCONUT MOUSSE

PREPARATION TIME 10 MIN

COOKING TIME 5 MIN

SERVINGS 22

INGREDIENTS:

- 2 and 3/4 cup coconut milk
- 1 teaspoon coconut extract
- 1 teaspoon vanilla extract
- 4 teaspoons coconut sugar
- 1 cup coconut, toasted

DIRECTIONS:

Prepare coconut milk with the coconut extract, vanilla extract, coconut and sugar in a bowl.

Whisk well, divide into small cups and serve cold.

Nutrition: Calories: 250 Total Fat: 18g Total Carbohydrates: 18g Fiber: 1g Sugar: 14g Protein: 3g

154. EASY CHOCOLATE PUDDING

PREPARATION TIME 10 MIN

COOKING TIME 10 MIN

SERVINGS 2

INGREDIENTS:

- 2 tablespoons coconut sugar
- 3 tablespoons cornstarch
- 2 tablespoons cocoa powder
- 2 cups almond milk
- 1/3 cup chocolate chips, unsweetened
- 1/2 teaspoon vanilla extract

DIRECTIONS:

Put the cornstarch in a pan, add cocoa, sugar and milk, whisk well and heat up over medium heat for 5 minutes.

Take this off heat, add vanilla and chocolate chips, whisk well, pour into small cups and serve cold.

Enjoy!

Nutrition: Calories: 93 Total Fat: 0.3g Total Carbohydrates: 21g Fiber: 0.3g Sugar: 15g Protein: 2g

155. BLUEBERRY ORANGE COMPOTE

PREPARATION TIME 10 MIN

COOKING TIME 15 MIN

SERVINGS 2

INGREDIENTS:

- 5 tablespoons coconut sugar
- 1-ounce orange juice
- 1-pound blueberries

DIRECTIONS:

In a pot, combine the sugar with the orange juice and blueberries then toss.

Bring to a boil over medium heat, cook for 15 minutes, divide into bowls and serve cold.

Enjoy!

Nutrition: Calories: 170 Total Fat: 2g Total Carbohydrates: 37g Fiber: 2g Sugar: 20g Protein: 0g

156. VANILLA APPLE MIX

PREPARATION TIME
10 MIN

COOKING TIME
15 MIN

SERVINGS
2

INGREDIENTS:

- 6 apples, cored and roughly chopped
- 4 tablespoons coconut sugar
- 2 teaspoons vanilla extract
- 2 teaspoons lemon juice
- 2 teaspoons cinnamon powder

DIRECTIONS:

In a small pan, combine the apples with the sugar, vanilla, lemon juice and cinnamon, toss.

Heat up over medium heat, cook for about 10-15 minutes.

Divide between small dessert plates and serve.

Nutrition: Calories: 70 Total Fat: 0g Total Carbohydrates: 16g Fiber: 1g Sugar: 10g Protein: 1g

157. NIGELLA MANGO MIX

PREPARATION TIME 10 MIN

COOKING TIME 10 MIN

SERVINGS 2

INGREDIENTS:

- 1/2-pounds mango, peeled and cubed
- 1 teaspoon nigella seeds
- 3 tablespoons coconut sugar
- 1/2 cup apple cider vinegar
- 1 teaspoon cinnamon powder

DIRECTIONS:

In a small pot, combine the mango with the nigella seeds, sugar, vinegar and cinnamon, toss.

Let it simmer over medium heat, cook for 10 minutes.

Divide into bowls and serve.

Nutrition: Calories: 212 Total Fat: 0g Total Carbohydrates: 5g Fiber: 0g Sugar: 20g Protein: 0g

158. ALMOND PEACH MIX

PREPARATION TIME
10 MIN

COOKING TIME
10 MIN

SERVINGS
2

INGREDIENTS:

- 4 cups water
- 1 peach, chopped
- 2 cups rolled oats
- 1 teaspoon vanilla extract
- 2 tablespoons flax meal
- 1/2 cup almonds, chopped

DIRECTIONS:

In a pan, combine the water with the oats, vanilla extract, flax meal, almonds and peach, stir well.

Wait for it to simmer over medium heat, cook for 10 minutes.

Divide into bowls and serve.

Nutrition: Calories: 250 Total Fat: 7g Total Carbohydrates: 50g Fiber: 6g Sugar: 15g Protein: 8g

159. EASY LEMON CREAM

PREPARATION TIME 10 MIN

COOKING TIME 15 MIN

SERVINGS 2

INGREDIENTS:

- 3 cups coconut milk
- Juice of 2 lemons
- Lemon zest of 2 lemons, grated
- 1/2 cup maple syrup
- 3 tablespoons coconut oil
- 1 egg
- 2 tablespoons gelatin
- 1 cup water

DIRECTIONS:

In your blender, mix coconut milk with lemon juice, lemon zest, maple syrup, coconut oil, egg and gelatin and pulse well.

Divide this into small jars and seal them.

Put the jars in a pan, add the water, introduce in the oven and cook at 380 degrees F for 15 minutes.

Serve the cream cold.

Nutrition: Calories: 72 Total Fat: 3g Total Carbohydrates: 12g Fiber: 0.5g Sugar: 10g Protein: 1g

PREPARATION TIME
10 MIN

COOKING TIME
15 MIN

SERVINGS
24

160. VANILLA PUMPKIN BARS

INGREDIENTS:
- 2 1/2 cups almond flour
- 1/2 teaspoon baking soda
- 1 tablespoon flax seed
- 3 tablespoons water
- 1/2 cup pumpkin flesh, mashed
- 1/4 cup coconut sugar
- 2 tablespoons coconut butter
- 1 teaspoon vanilla extract

DIRECTIONS:

In a bowl, mix flax seed with water and stir.

Get another bowl, mix flour with baking soda, flax meal, pumpkin, coconut sugar, coconut butter and vanilla, stir well.

Spread on a baking sheet, press well, bake in the oven at 350 degrees F for 15 minutes.

Leave aside to cool down, cut into bars and serve.

Nutrition: Calories: 130 Total Fat: 7g Total Carbohydrates: 15g Fiber: 0.4g Sugar: 10g Protein: 1.3g

CHAPTER 5. DASH DIET HEALTHY RECIPES FOR BEGINNERS

BREAKFAST

161. BUCKWHEAT CREPES

PREPARATION TIME 1 H

COOKING TIME 10 MIN

SERVINGS 2

INGREDIENTS:

- 2 1/4 cups buckwheat flour (300g)
- 750 ml of water (3 cups)
- 1 egg (flax-egg, if vegan)
- Butter or coconut oil
- 1/2 tsp. salt
- Shallots, mushrooms, garlic, nutmeg, and oregano (optional)

DIRECTIONS:

Add the buckwheat flour, egg, water, and salt to a blender and mix it until smooth.

Cover this batter and let it sit in the refrigerator overnight or for at least 2 hours.

When you take out the mixture, make sure the consistency resembles that of melted ice cream.

Heat the crepe pan and grease it with 1/4 tsp. butter or coconut oil.

Pour 1/3 cup batter into the pan and spread it thinly by rotating the pan.

Keep flipping both sides for 1 to 2 minutes to brown it up. Repeat the process.

Stir-fry the shallots, mushrooms, garlic, and nutmeg with oregano and put it inside the crepes.

Nutrition: Calories: 101 Total Fat: 6g Total Carbohydrates: 9g Fiber: 1g Sugar: 0.4g Protein: 4g

162. PUMPKIN GRANOLA YOGURT PARFAIT

PREPARATION TIME 10 MIN

COOKING TIME 30 MIN

SERVINGS 2

INGREDIENTS:

- 5 cups rolled oats; if you want to add nuts, add 3 cups oats and 1 cup nuts
- 1/2 tsp. salt
- 1/2 tsp. pumpkin pie spice
- 1 1/2 tsp. cinnamon
- 1/4 cup brown sugar
- 1/2 cup honey
- 1 tsp. vanilla
- 1/3 cup coconut oil
- Light pumpkin pie yogurt
- 3 tbsp. canned pumpkin

DIRECTIONS:

Mix the pumpkin puree, oats, spice, honey, vanilla, maple syrup, and cinnamon in a bowl.

Heat a pan for about 15 minutes and then add the mixture to the pan.

Bake the mixture until it is golden brown. Bake in 15-minutes intervals and stir at every interval.

Allow it to cool completely. You may even freeze it as well. When you cool the food, it becomes even tastier.

Serve it with yogurt and granola layers. Enjoy.

Nutrition: Calories: 208 Total Fat: 2g Total Carbohydrates: 41g Fiber: 4g Sugar: 20g Protein: 8g

163. SWEET POTATO OAT WAFFLES

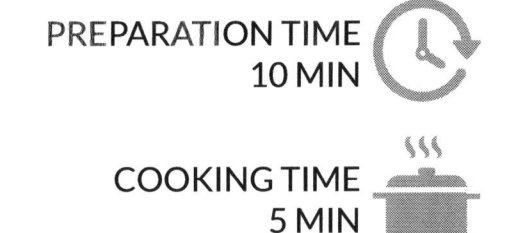

PREPARATION TIME
10 MIN

COOKING TIME
5 MIN

SERVINGS
2

INGREDIENTS:

- cooked large sweet potato
- 1 cooked large sweet potato
- 1/2 cup flour
- 1/2 cup oats
- 2 eggs
- 1/2 cup almond milk
- 3/4 tsp. cinnamon
- 1 tsp. baking powder
- 1/4 tsp. salt
- Cooking spray

DIRECTIONS:

Set the waffle maker to preheat before you start making the waffles.

Take a jar for blending and add all the ingredients to it. The process is as instructed here. After that, wait until the mixture is blended and forms a puree.

Set the batter aside for about 10 minutes, as this will give you the best results. Letting it rest will give it a nutty, sweet potato flavor.

Pour the batter into the mold. Make sure the batter fills about 1/3 of the mold to make the perfect waffle.

When the indicator on the waffle iron turns green, cook the waffles for an additional 30 seconds. You can cook them for 4 to 5 minutes per batch.

Serve the waffles with maple syrup, whipped cream, pecans, or anything else as desired.

Nutrition: Calories: 160 Total Fat: 5g Total Carbohydrates: 25g Fiber: 1g Sugar: 4g Protein: 3g

164. FRENCH TOAST

PREPARATION TIME 10 MIN

COOKING TIME 6 MIN

SERVINGS 2

INGREDIENTS:

- 2 large eggs
- 1 large egg white
- 1/2 cup 2% milk
- 1 tbsp. butter, melted
- 1 tbsp. honey
- 1 tbsp. sugar
- 1/2 tsp. ground cinnamon
- 1/4 tsp. salt
- Nonstick cooking spray
- 1/4 tsp. vanilla extract
- 8 slices of light bread

DIRECTIONS:

In a wide mixing bowl, add egg white, milk, sugar, butter, honey, and vanilla extract along with salt. Whip using a whipper.

On a non-stick skillet or large griddle, spray some nonstick cooking spray and keep it on a low flame.

Dip the pieces of bread into the mixing bowl and place them on the skillet. Ensure that you have coated both sides of the bread with the mixture. You can place as much bread on the skillet as you want, but make sure they fit properly without overlapping each other.

Fry the bread over a medium flame until it is golden brown. Fry at least 3 minutes or more if required.

Serve the French toast hot and garnish with fresh berries. You can also pour pure maple syrup on top of the bread to enhance the taste.

Nutrition: Calories: 165 Total Fat: 3g Total Carbohydrates: 27g Fiber: 2g Sugar: 3g Protein: 5g

165. OPEN FACE BREAKFAST SANDWICH

PREPARATION TIME
5 MIN

COOKING TIME
10 MIN

SERVINGS
2

INGREDIENTS:

- 2 slices of bread
- 4 rashers of bacon
- 2 eggs
- tbsp. milk
- 1/2 sliced tomato
- 4 heaping tbsp. guacamole: 1/2 sliced avocado, 1/2 mashed avocado
- Pepper to taste
- Cilantro for garnish

DIRECTIONS:

Put slices of bread in an oven or toaster until they are crisp and brown.

Cook the bacon over medium heat and drain the excess oil using paper towels. Once it is cooled, chop the bacon into small pieces.

Get another bowl, beat eggs and the milk together. Fry the eggs sunny side up and add salt and pepper as per taste.

Spread avocado on the bread slices

Top with the eggs and add diced tomatoes on top.

You can add cilantro for a garnish along with the chopped bacon.

Your sandwich is ready. Serve it hot for breakfast and get ready for the day with delicious food.

Nutrition: Calories: 300 Total Fat: 19g Total Carbohydrates: 16g Fiber: 3g Sugar: 2g Protein: 15g

PREPARATION TIME
5 MIN

COOKING TIME
30 MIN

SERVINGS
2

166. POTATO SALAD SIDE DISH

INGREDIENTS:
- 1-pound potatoes
- 1 large yellow onion
- 1 large carrot
- 2 ribs of celery
- 2 tablespoons of minced fresh dill
- 1 teaspoon of ground black pepper
- 1/4 cup of low-calorie mayonnaise
- 1 tablespoon of Dijon mustard
- 1 tablespoon of red wine vinegar

DIRECTIONS:
Dice and boil potatoes

Chop the yellow onion

Dice carrot and celery

Pour potatoes into a bowl with onion, carrot and celery

Add fresh dill, mayonnaise, black pepper, mustard and vinegar. Mix thoroughly.

Serve chilled.

Nutrition: Calories: 108 Total Fat: 5g Total Carbohydrates: 12g Fiber: 0g Sugar: 0g Proteins: 1g

167. BROCCOLI WITH GARLIC AND LEMON

PREPARATION TIME
5 MIN

COOKING TIME
5 MIN

SERVINGS
2

INGREDIENTS:

- 4 cups of broccoli
- 1 teaspoon of olive oil
- 1 tablespoon of minced garlic
- 1 teaspoon of lemon zest
- 1/4 teaspoon of kosher salt
- 1/4 teaspoon of ground black pepper

DIRECTIONS:

Prepare a saucepan with a cup of water and boil.

Add broccoli to boiling water.

Cook until tender and drain.

Heat oil in pan under medium heat.

Add garlic and stir for 30 seconds

Add broccoli, salt, lemon zest and pepper

Nutrition: Calories: 50 Total Fat: 1g Total Carbohydrates: 7g Fiber: 2g Sugar: 0g Protein: 2g

168. CAULIFLOWER MASHED POTATOES

PREPARATION TIME 5 MIN

COOKING TIME 5-10 MIN

SERVINGS 2

INGREDIENTS:
- 1 garlic clove
- 1 head of cauliflower
- 1 white leek (split into 4)
- 1 tablespoon of margarine
- 1/2 teaspoon of pepper

DIRECTIONS:

Steam cauliflower, garlic and leeks in hot water until tender

Use blender to grind the vegetables

Mix with margarine and pepper

Nutrition: Calories: 65 Total Fat: 3g Total Carbohydrates: 9g Fiber: 3g Sugar: 0g Protein: 2g

169. GREEN BEANS WITH RED PEPPER & GARLIC

PREPARATION TIME
5 MIN

COOKING TIME
5 MIN

SERVINGS
2

INGREDIENTS:

- 1 pound of green beans
- 2 teaspoon of olive oil
- 1 red bell pepper
- 1/2 teaspoon of chili paste
- 1 garlic clove
- 1 teaspoon of sesame oil
- 1/4 teaspoon of salt
- 1/4 teaspoon of ground black pepper

DIRECTIONS:

Boil green beans in hot water until tender-crisp

Heat olive oil in a saucepan

Add bell pepper and stir for a minute

Add green beans and stir for a minute

Add chili paste and garlic and stir for a minute

Sprinkle salt and pepper

Drizzle with sesame oil

Nutrition: Calories: 60 Total Fat: 2g Total Carbohydrates: 9g Fiber: 3g Sugar: 4g Protein: 2g

PREPARATION TIME
5 MIN

COOKING TIME
8 MIN

SERVINGS
2

170. HONEY SAGE CARROTS

INGREDIENTS:

- 2 cups of sliced carrots
- 2 teaspoons of butter
- 2 tablespoons of honey
- 1 tablespoon of fresh sage
- 1/4 teaspoon of ground black pepper
- 1/8 teaspoon of salt

DIRECTIONS:

Boil carrots in hot water for 5 minutes

Preheat pan and add butter

Add carrots, honey, sage, pepper and salt to hot butter

Stir for 3 minutes

Serve warm

Nutrition: Calories: 74 Total Fat: 2g Total Carbohydrates: 15g Fiber: 2g Sugar: 12g Protein: 1g

SALADS

171. CHICKEN SALAD

PREPARATION TIME
10 MIN

COOKING TIME
10-15 MIN

SERVINGS
2

INGREDIENTS:

- 4 boneless, skinless chicken breasts
- 1 tablespoon olive oil
- 1 cup pineapple, diced
- 2 cups broccoli florets
- 4 cups spinach, chopped
- 1/2 cup red onion, diced finely
- 1/4 cup olive oil
- 2 tablespoons balsamic vinegar
- 1 teaspoon honey

DIRECTIONS:

Cut the chicken breasts into cubes, then place them in a large, nonstick skillet with 1 tablespoon olive oil. Cook the chicken for 8-10 minutes.

Then, in a large bowl, mix the cooked chicken, pineapple, broccoli florets, spinach and red onions. Set aside.

For the dressing, mix well the olive oil, honey, and balsamic vinegar. Put the dressing over the salad greens and combine well.

Nutrition: Calories: 240 Total Fat: 11g Total Carbohydrates: 17g Fiber: 3g Sugar: 3g Protein: 34g

PREPARATION TIME
10 MIN

COOKING TIME
5 MIN

SERVINGS
2

172. ASIAN VEGGIE SALAD WITH SNOW PEAS

INGREDIENTS:

- 1/2 cups carrots, diced
- 1/2 cups red bell pepper, diced
- 1/2 cups bok choy
- 1 1/2 cups spinach
- 1 cup red cabbage
- 3 cloves garlic, minced
- 1 tablespoon fresh cilantro, chopped
- 1/2 tablespoons Cashews, chopped
- 1/2 cups snow peas
- 2 teaspoons sesame oil
- 2 teaspoons low-sodium soy sauce

DIRECTIONS:

Put all vegetables to a mixing bowl, then add the minced garlic, cilantro, and cashews.

Mix the sesame oil and low-sodium soy sauce in a small bowl, and then pour the mixture over the salad.

Combine well and serve.

Nutrition: Calories: 107 Total Fat: 8g Total Carbohydrates: 5g Fiber: 3g Sugar: 2g Protein: 4g

173. BAKED COD WITH A CITRUS TWIST

PREPARATION TIME 10 MIN

COOKING TIME 20 MIN

SERVINGS 2

INGREDIENTS:

- 2 pieces baked cod
- 1/2 tablespoons olive oil
- 1 1/2 cups spinach, chopped
- 1 1/2 cups kohlrabi, chopped
- 1 cup celery, diced
- 1 1/2 cups carrots, diced
- 2 tablespoons fresh basil, chopped
- 1 tablespoon fresh parsley, chopped
- 3/4 cup red bell pepper, diced
- 1 teaspoon black pepper
- 3 cloves garlic, minced
- 1 lemon, juiced and zest
- 1 lime, juiced and zest
- 1 grapefruit, sliced
- 1 orange, sliced

DIRECTIONS:

Place the two pieces of cod on a baking sheet and drizzle the fish with olive oil. Bake for 20 minutes at 350 degrees Fahrenheit.

Add the remaining ingredients to a large mixing bowl and combine thoroughly.

Once the cod is finished, divide the salad into two equal portions.

Lay one piece of cod on top of each salad.

Nutrition: Calories: 189 Total Fat: 6g Total Carbohydrates: 10g Fiber: 1g Sugar: 1g Protein: 22g

174. THE MIGHTY TABBOULEH SALAD

PREPARATION TIME
10 MIN

COOKING TIME
15-20 MIN

SERVINGS
2

INGREDIENTS:

- 1/2 cups water
- 3/4 cup bulgur
- 1 tomato, diced
- 1 cup fresh parsley, chopped
- 3 medium green onions, chopped
- 1 teaspoon dill weed
- 1/8 cup black olives, chopped
- 1/4 cup raisins
- 1/4 cup lemon juice
- 2 tablespoons olive oil
- 1 teaspoon black pepper

DIRECTIONS:

Boil a water in a small saucepan. Add the bulgur.

Remove the saucepan from the heat and cover it. Let it stand for 15-20 minutes.

Once it absorbed all of the water, add the bulgur to a large mixing bowl, then add the remaining ingredients.

Stir to combine and serve.

Nutrition: Calories: 62 Total Fat: 2g Total Carbohydrates: 6g Fiber: 0g Sugar: 3g Protein: 2g

175. GREEK SALAD WITH FETA CRUMBLES

PREPARATION TIME 10 MIN

COOKING TIME 25 MIN

SERVINGS 2

INGREDIENTS:

- 1 tablespoon red wine vinegar
- 1 tablespoon fresh lemon juice
- 2 teaspoons fresh oregano, chopped
- 1/2 teaspoon salt
- 1/2 teaspoon black pepper
- 12 cups spinach, chopped
- 1 eggplant, peeled and cubed
- 1 cucumber, diced
- 1 tomato, diced
- 1/2 red onion, diced
- 1/8 cup black olives
- 2 tablespoons feta cheese, crumbled

DIRECTIONS:

Preheat your oven to 450 degrees Fahrenheit and place the cubed eggplant on a baking sheet. Bake the eggplant for 10 minutes, then stir, then bake for 10 more minutes.

In a small bowl, combine the red wine vinegar, lemon juice, oregano, salt and pepper.

In a larger mixing bowl, combine the remaining ingredients except for the feta cheese and black olives.

Add dressing over the salad and combine. Whenever the eggplant cubes are done, add them to the salad and stir.

When ready to serve, sprinkle the black olives and feta cheese over the salad.

Nutrition: Calories: 106 Total Fat: 7g Total Carbohydrates: 3g Fiber: 0g Sugar: 0g Protein: 6g

SOUPS

176. ZUCCHINI SOUP

PREPARATION TIME
10 MIN

COOKING TIME
15 MIN

SERVINGS
2

INGREDIENTS:

- 4 cups zucchini, cubed
- 1 medium onion, diced
- 2 cans fat-free low-sodium chicken broth (14 oz.)
- 2 tablespoons margarine or butter
- 1/2 cup of skim milk
- 1 dash nutmeg
- salt and pepper to taste

DIRECTIONS:

Slice the zucchini into cubes and diced the onion.

Warm the pot over medium heat, put some cooking spray.

Put the onions and cook until they start to turn translucent.

Add chicken broth and zucchini.

Increase to medium/high heat.

Cook 10-15 minutes, until zucchini is tender.

In batches if necessary, puree mixture in blender and return to pot.

Add butter, 1/2 cup of milk, and dash of nutmeg.

Season to taste with salt and pepper.

Nutrition: Calories: 130 Total Fat: 4g Total Carbohydrates: 20g Fiber: 4g Sugar: 0g Protein: 5g

177. CREAMY PUMPKIN SOUP

PREPARATION TIME 10 MIN

COOKING TIME 20 MIN

SERVINGS 2

INGREDIENTS:

- 1 tablespoon red wine vinegar
- 1 tablespoon red wine vinegar
- 1 onion, chopped
- 1 kg pumpkin flesh, chopped
- 1 carrot
- 3 sprigs fresh rosemary
- 4 cups low sodium chicken stock or 4 cups vegetable stock
- 3 bay leaves
- 1 cup skim milk powder

DIRECTIONS:

Warm the oil in a saucepan. Add and cook onion for 3 minutes.

Put the pumpkin, carrot and rosemary. Cook and stir for more minutes.

Put the stock and bay leaves. Wait for it to boil.

Put cover and simmer for until vegetables are tender.

Take any bay leaves and rosemary stalks.

Prepare the soup in the blender with skim milk powder and puree. Transfer into a bowl.

Put back into the saucepan, heat through and serve.

Nutrition: Calories: 162 Total Fat: 9g Total Carbohydrates: 18g Fiber: 5g Sugar: 7g Protein: 5g

178. HOME MADE TOMATO SOUP

PREPARATION TIME 10 MIN

COOKING TIME 20 MIN

SERVINGS 2

INGREDIENTS:

- 2 tablespoons olive oil
- 1 tbsp. balsamic vinegar
- 1 yellow or white onion, chopped
- 3 cloves garlic, minced
- 2 pounds tomatoes, deseeded, chopped
- 1/4 teaspoon red pepper flakes
- 1 tablespoon brown sugar
- 1/2 teaspoon dried thyme
- 4 small slices white bread, crust removed
- 1 1/2 cup vegetable stock or low-sodium chicken
- black pepper

DIRECTIONS:

Add and warm oil in a large saucepan or stockpot.

Add the onions and garlic; sauté for 5 minutes.

Put tomatoes, then pepper, sugar, thyme and bread. Let it cook for 3 minutes.

Transfer in a food processor or blender. Mix well.

Carefully put the stock and let it boil for 10 minutes.

Put vinegar and cook another two minutes.

Nutrition: Calories: 52 Total Fat: 0g Total Carbohydrates: 9g Fiber: 0g Sugar: 9g Protein: 0g

179. SAVORY TOMATO LENTIL SOUP

PREPARATION TIME
10 MIN

COOKING TIME
30 MIN

SERVINGS
2

INGREDIENTS:

- garlic as much as desired, minced
- 1 medium onion, diced
- 3 medium carrots, diced
- 2 tbsp olive oil
- 2 stalks celery, chopped
- 6 cups vegetable stock
- 1 28-oz can dice tomatoes, including juice or 5-8 diced fresh
- tomatoes with 1/4 cup water
- 2 cups cooked or canned lentils
- pepper (to taste)
- cayenne pepper (to taste)
- 1 cup dry pasta

DIRECTIONS:

Sauté garlic, onions, and carrots until the translucent.

Add the celery, stock, tomatoes, lentils, pepper, and cayenne and bring to a boil.

Reduce heat to low and simmer for 20 minutes or until carrots are tender.

Add pasta and simmer to 10 more minutes before serving.

Nutrition: Calories: 140 Total Fat: 0g Total Carbohydrates: 27g Fiber: 6g Sugar: 5g Protein: 8g

180. CREAMY BUTTERNUT SQUASH SOUP

PREPARATION TIME 10 MIN

COOKING TIME 30 MIN

SERVINGS 2

INGREDIENTS:

- 2 1/4 lbs. butternut squash
- 1 cup chopped onion
- 1 tablespoon grated fresh ginger
- 1 tablespoon unsalted butter
- 3 cups low sodium vegetable broth (or chicken broth)

DIRECTIONS:

Preheat oven to 450F.

Slice squash in half lengthwise, take out the seeds and place cut side down on a baking sheet.

Roast the squash until it's tender. Wait for it to cool.

While the squash is roasting, sauté the ginger and onion in the butter until soft.

Put the broth, then cover and let it cook for 10 minutes.

Prepare the squash by taking it from the skin.

Put half squash and half broth in a blender, mix until smooth.

Repeat with the remaining. If needed, put some water to achieve the desired consistency.

Return the soup to the saucepan and reheat.

Salt and pepper to taste.

Nutrition: Calories: 160 Total Fat: 11g Total Carbohydrates: 0g Fiber: 0g Sugar: 8g Protein: 0g

VEGAN AND VEGETARIAN

181. TOMATOES, ASPARAGUS AND GOAT CHEESE PENNE

PREPARATION TIME 5 MIN

COOKING TIME 30 MIN

SERVINGS 2

INGREDIENTS:

- 1/3-pound whole-wheat penne pasta
- 1/2 cup chopped asparagus, 1-inch pieces
- 1 tablespoon water
- 1/2 cup halved cherry tomatoes
- 1/4 cup chopped fresh basil, plus whole leaves for garnish
- 1 tablespoon minced garlic
- 1/8 teaspoon freshly ground black pepper
- 2 ounces goat cheese

DIRECTIONS:

Fill a large pot 3/4 full of water and boil. Add pasta and cook until al dente (tender), 10 to 12 minutes, or according to the package Directions:. Drain pasta.

While pasta is cooking, put asparagus and water in a microwave-safe bowl. Heat asparagus on high until tender-crisp, about 3 minutes.

Combine cherry tomatoes, basil, garlic and pepper in a bowl. Add asparagus, pasta and goat cheese and toss until well-mixed. Place in the refrigerator for at least 20 minutes to cool.

Divide pasta between the plates and garnish with fresh basil leaves.

Nutrition: Calories: 390 Total Fat: 8g Total Carbohydrates: 60g Fiber: 10g Sugar: 0g Protein: 17g

PREPARATION TIME
5 MIN

COOKING TIME
20 MIN

SERVINGS
2

182. GARDEN QUESADILLAS

INGREDIENTS:

- 2 small green and/or red sweet peppers, cut into thin strips
- 1 small red onion, cut into thin 1-inch-long strips
- 2 teaspoons olive oil or canola oil
- 1/2 teaspoon ground cumin
- 1/2 teaspoon chili powder
- 2 tablespoons fresh cilantro
- 1/3 cup fat free cream cheese
- 5 flour tortillas (6 inch)
- 1/4 cup salsa, if desired

DIRECTIONS:

Cook sweet peppers and onion in 1 teaspoon of the oil in a large non-stick skillet 3 to 5 minutes, or until crisp-tender. Stir in cumin and chili powder.

Cook and stir for another minute. Stir in cilantro. Set vegetables aside.

Spread cream cheese over half of one side of each tortilla. Top with pepper mix. Fold tortilla in half over peppers and press gently.

Place tortillas on large baking sheet and brush with remaining oil. Bake in a 425°F (220°C) oven for 5 minutes.

Cut each quesadilla into 4 wedges. Serve warm. Top with salsa, if desired.

Nutrition: Calories: 102 Total Fat: 4g Total Carbohydrates: 15g Fiber: 3g Sugar: 0.5g Protein: 3g

183. BEAN BARLEY BURGERS

PREPARATION TIME
10 MIN

COOKING TIME
20 MIN

SERVINGS
2

INGREDIENTS:

- 1/2 teaspoon garlic powder
- 2 cups kidney beans cooked
- 1/2 cup wheat germ
- 1 tablespoon olive oil
- 1/2 cup onion chopped
- 3 garlic cloves, minced
- 1 teaspoon sea salt
- 1/2 teaspoon sage
- 1/2 teaspoon celery seed, ground
- 2 cups whole hull-less barley, cooked

DIRECTIONS:

Cook beans and barley according to package instructions until soft. Mash beans and barley together.

Fry onion and garlic in oil until golden. Add bean/barley mix along with spices and wheat germ. Stir to combine.

Form into 4" patties and fry on medium heat until brown on both sides.

Makes about 8 burgers.

Nutrition: Calories: 210 Total Fat: 8g Total Carbohydrates: 29g Fiber: 6g Sugar: 3g Protein: 8g

PREPARATION TIME
10 MIN

COOKING TIME
20 MIN

SERVINGS
2

184. SOUTHWESTERN VEGETABLES TACO

INGREDIENTS:

- 1 tablespoon olive oil
- 1 medium red onion, chopped (about 1 cup)
- 1 cup diced yellow summer squash
- 1 cup diced green zucchini
- 3 large garlic cloves, minced
- 4 medium tomatoes, seeded and chopped
- 1 jalapeno chili, seeded and chopped
- 1 cup fresh corn kernels (cut from about 2 ears of corn) or 1 cup frozen corn
- 1 cup canned pinto or black beans, rinsed and drained
- 1/2 cup chopped fresh cilantro
- 8 corn tortillas
- 1/2 cup smoke-flavored salsa

DIRECTIONS:

Put olive oil over medium heat in a large saucepan.

Add onion and cook until soft. Add the summer squash and zucchini and continue cooking about 5 minutes or until tender.

Stir in the garlic, tomatoes, jalapeno, corn kernels and beans. Cook until vegetables are tender-crisp, about 5 minutes. Add cilantro and remove from the heat.

Over medium heat, heat a large frying pan. Add 1 tortilla to pan and heat until softened, about 20 seconds per side. Repeat with the remaining tortillas.

Divide tortillas among individual plates. Scoop an equal amount of vegetable mix on each tortilla.

Top each with 2 tablespoons of the salsa.

Nutrition: Calories: 300 Total Fat: 4g Total Carbohydrates: 50g Fiber: 26g Sugar: 8g Protein: 11g

185. ROTELLE PASTA WITH SUN-DRIED TOMATO AND BLACK OLIVE SAUCE

PREPARATION TIME 10 MIN

COOKING TIME 25 MIN

SERVINGS 2

INGREDIENTS:

- 2 tablespoons olive oil
- 4 garlic cloves, mashed
- 1/3 cup dry-packed sun-dried tomatoes, soaked in water to rehydrate, drained and chopped
- 1 3/4 cups unsalted vegetable broth
- 8 ounces uncooked whole-wheat rotelle pasta
- 1/2 cup sliced black olives (about 15 medium olives)
- 1/2 cup chopped fresh parsley
- 4 teaspoons Parmesan cheese

DIRECTIONS:

Heat olive oil and garlic over medium heat in a large skillet. Stir in the sun-dried tomatoes and unsalted vegetable broth. Reduce heat, cover and simmer for 10 minutes.

Boil a large pot 3/4 full of water. Add pasta and cook until al dente, 10 to 12 minutes, or according to the package Directions:. Drain pasta.

Add olives and parsley to the sun-dried tomato mix. Stir to combine.

Divide pasta among individual plates. Top each with 1/4 of the sun-dried tomato mixture and 1 teaspoon Parmesan cheese.

Nutrition: Calories: 320 Total Fat: 10g Total Carbohydrates: 45g Fiber: 6g Sugar: 5g Protein: 10g

FISH AND SEAFOOD

186. SCALLOP & VEG SKEWERS

PREPARATION TIME 10 MIN

COOKING TIME 25 MIN

SERVINGS 2

INGREDIENTS:

- 1 lb. of scallops
- 1 tbsp olive oil
- Juice from half of a lemon
- 1/2 tsp thyme
- 2 shallots, peeled and halved
- 2 bell peppers, cut into thick chunks
- 6 cherry tomatoes
- 1/2 zucchini, cut into chunks
- Ground black pepper, to taste
- Skewers, soaked in water

DIRECTIONS:

In a bowl combine the oil, lemon juice, thyme and pepper. Mix well before adding the scallops and covering. Leave the scallops in the marinade for 20 minutes.

While the scallops marinade preheats your broiler/grill.

Skewer the vegetables and scallops in an alternating fashion.

Season with pepper.

Place under the heat source and cook for about 3 minutes per side.

Nutrition: Calories: 400 Total Fat: 25g Total Carbohydrates: 18g Fiber: 2g Sugar: 5g Protein: 30g

187. HONEY SCALLOPS

PREPARATION TIME 10 MIN

COOKING TIME 15 MIN

SERVINGS 2

INGREDIENTS:

- 1 lb. of scallops
- 4 tbsp honey
- 2 tbsp lime juice
- 3 tbsp olive oil
- 2 bell peppers, chopped
- 1 onion, chopped
- 1 courgette, chopped
- 2 cups of spinach

DIRECTIONS:

Preheat your broiler/grill. Position the rack around 4-5" from the heat source.

Lay foil over a baking tray and grease with 1 tbsp of olive oil.

Add the honey, lime juice and 1 tbsp olive oil to a bowl, whisk together.

Put the scallops and gently toss to coat. Leave to marinade for 5 minutes.

Place a pan over a medium heat and add the remaining olive oil.

Add the onion, courgette and peppers once heated, cook for 5 minutes stirring frequently.

Put the spinach to the pan and cook for a further 2 minutes. Take off the heat and set aside.

Lay the scallops out on the baking sheet and then place under the heat for 4 minutes.

Flip to other side then cook for a further 2 minutes.

Serve up the vegetables and lay the scallops over the top. Pour the remaining juices over the dish as a sauce.

Nutrition: Calories: 131 Total Fat: 1g Total Carbohydrates: 3g Fiber: 0g Sugar: 0.1g Protein: 19g

188. RED ONION SALMON

PREPARATION TIME 10 MIN

COOKING TIME 30 MIN

SERVINGS 2

INGREDIENTS:

- 4 salmon fillets
- 3 cloves of garlic, minced
- 2 red onions, finely chopped
- 2 tbsp olive oil
- 2 tsp ground cayenne
- 1 cup of uncooked brown rice

DIRECTIONS:

Preheat your oven to 375F.

Cook the rice per package instructions. While the rice cooks move onto the next step.

In a bowl mix the garlic and onion.

Take a large baking dish and lay out the red onion along the bottom creating a base layer.

Sprinkle 1 tsp of the cayenne over the onion and then lay the salmon fillets, skin side down, onto the onion.

Put olive oil over everything and then sprinkle the remaining cayenne over the dish.

Cover and put in the oven for 18-20 minutes.

Serve the salmon over the cooked rice and use the juices from the dish as a sauce.

Nutrition: Calories: 410 Total Fat: 18g Total Carbohydrates: 17g Fiber: 5g Sugar: 0.1g Protein: 46g

189. HALIBUT IN A SPICED SALSA

PREPARATION TIME 10 MIN

COOKING TIME 15 MIN

SERVINGS 2

INGREDIENTS:

- 4 fillets of halibut
- 2 large tomatoes, diced
- 2 tbsp basil, chopped
- 1 tsp oregano, chopped
- 1 tbsp minced garlic
- 3 tsp of ground paprika
- 3 tsp olive oil
- 1 bag of mixed salad

DIRECTIONS:

Preheat your oven to 350F.

Put 1 teaspoon olive oil to the baking tray and set aside.

Mix the tomato, garlic, paprika, oregano, olive oil and basil in a bowl.

Lay the fish out on the baking tray and spoon the tomato mixture over each fillet.

Put in the oven and bake for 13-15 minutes.

Serve with a mixed salad.

Nutrition: Calories: 290 Total Fat: 8g Total Carbohydrates: 19g Fiber: 3g Sugar: 0g Protein: 37g

190. HALIBUT WITH A PEA PUREE

PREPARATION TIME 10 MIN

COOKING TIME 20 MIN

SERVINGS 2

INGREDIENTS:

- 2 halibut fillets
- 5 oz. of frozen peas
- 1 & 1/2 tsp basil
- Ground black pepper, to taste
- 1/2 tsp olive oil
- 8 baby potatoes, chopped
- 2 tbsp of olive oil

DIRECTIONS:

Preheat your oven to 400F.

Let the peas defrost and then add to a blender, along with the basil and pepper. Pulse until smooth.

Place a pan over a low heat. Add the pea puree and heat while stirring occasionally.

Place another pan over a medium-high heat and add the olive oil. Put the fish with the skin side down and cook for 2 minutes.

Carefully remove from the pan, add to a baking dish and place in the oven for 8 minutes.

While the fish is cooking, put the chopped potatoes to the pan and sauté for 8 minutes, tossing frequently.

Season with black pepper.

Serve the pea puree drizzled over the fish and potatoes, season with more pepper to taste.

Nutrition: Calories: 420 Total Fat: 20g Total Carbohydrates: 18g Fiber: 5g Sugar: 0g Protein: 40g

POULTRY & MEAT

191. BREADED AND BAKED CHICKEN TENDERS

PREPARATION TIME 10 MIN

COOKING TIME 20 MIN

SERVINGS 2

INGREDIENTS:

- Nonstick cooking spray
- 1/4 cup whole wheat flour
- 1/4 teaspoon salt 2 large eggs
- 1 cup dried unseasoned breadcrumbs
- 1/4 cup grated Parmesan cheese
- 1/4 teaspoon paprika
- 1/4 teaspoon garlic powder
- 1-pound chicken tenders

DIRECTIONS:

Preheat the oven to 400°F.

Put a large sheet pan with foil and coat with nonstick cooking spray.

In a shallow dish, mix the flour and a small bowl, beat the eggs.

Get a second dish, mix the bread cru Parmesan, paprika, and garlic.

Soak each tender in the flour mixture, then the egg washes, then the bread mixture until covered on both sides. Arrange the tender with the prepared sheet pan.

Bake until the coating is golden brown, and the chicken is no longer pink in the center, turning once halfway through.

Nutrition: Calories: 320 Total Fat: 15g Total Carbohydrates: 21g Fiber: 1g Sugar: 0.8g Protein: 31g

PREPARATION TIME
5 MIN

COOKING TIME
30 MIN

SERVINGS
2

192. SAVORY PORK LOIN

INGREDIENTS:

- Nonstick cooking spray (optional)
- 2 lbs. boneless pork loin
- 1 1/2 tablespoons chopped fresh rosemary
- 1 1/2 tablespoons fresh thyme, chopped
- 2 garlic cloves, minced
- 1/4 tsp. ground black pepper

DIRECTIONS:

Preheat the oven to 350°F.

Prepare a roasting pan with aluminum foil or with nonstick cooking spray.

In a small bowl, mix the rosemary, thyme, garlic, and pepper. Season the pork loin with this rub.

Transfer to the prepared roasting pan and bake for 25 to 30 minutes, or the pork loin's internal temperature has reached 145°F.

Let rest for minutes before slicing. Portion the pork into 6 storage containers.

Nutrition: Calories: 227 Total Fat: 9g Total Carbohydrates: 8g Fiber: 1g Sugar: 2g Protein: 28g

193. HONEY-GARLIC PORK CHOPS

PREPARATION TIME: 5 MIN

COOKING TIME: 20 MIN

SERVINGS: 2

INGREDIENTS:

- 2 1/2 tablespoons honey 4 garlic cloves, minced
- 1 tablespoon reduced-sodium soy sauce 1 tablespoon no-salt-added ketchup
- 1/2 teaspoon freshly ground black pepper
- 1/2 teaspoon dried oregano
- 4 (6-ounce) bone-in loin pork chops, fat trimmed 1 tablespoon extra-virgin olive oil
- 1 tablespoon unsalted butter

DIRECTIONS:

Preheat the oven to 400°F.

Mix honey, garlic, soy sauce, ketchup, pepper, and oregano in a mixing bowl.

Add pork chops in a bowl and pour the sauce over them. Mix fully coated.

Prepare a large oven-safe skillet, heat the oil over medium-high heat.

Add the chops with sauce to the skillet. Cook 2 minutes per side, until brown slightly. Remove from the heat.

Add 3/4 teaspoon of butter to the top of each pork chop. Transfer to the o and bake for 15 to 18 minutes, or until the pork reaches an internal temperature of 145°F.

Let cool, then place a chop in each of 4 storage Containers. Divide the pan sauce evenly over the portions.

Nutrition: Calories: 204 Total Fat: 6g Total Carbohydrates: 18g Fiber: 0.2g Sugar: 16g Protein: 20g

194. BEEF TENDERLOIN MEDALLIONS WITH HORSERADISH YOGURT SAUCE

- **PREPARATION TIME** 10 MIN
- **COOKING TIME** 10 MIN
- **SERVINGS** 2

INGREDIENTS:

For The Horseradish Sauce
- 3/4 cup whole-milk Greek yogurt
- 2 tablespoons prepared horseradish 1 garlic clove, minced
- 1/4 teaspoon freshly ground black pepper 2 teaspoons 1% milk

For The Medallions
- 12 ounces beef tenderloin, flattened and cut into 4 pieces
- 1/2 teaspoon freshly ground black pepper
- 1/2 teaspoon garlic powder
- 1 tablespoon unsalted butter

DIRECTIONS:

To Make The Horseradish Sauce

Mix well the yogurt, horseradish, garlic, pepper, milk in a bowl. Divide the sauce among 4 condiment cups.

To Make The Medallions. Season the tenderloin with the pepper and garlic powder.

In a large skillet, melt the butter over medium-high heat. Add the beef a sauté for about 2 minutes on each side, or until the outside is browned, and the inside is very pink, medium-rare.

Remove from the heat. When cool, put the beef into 4 storage containers.

To serve, reheat the beef and top with horseradish sauce.

Nutrition: Calories: 240 Total Fat: 11g Total Carbohydrates: 2g Fiber: 0.2g Sugar: 2g Protein: 32g

195. GREEK-STYLE TOP ROUND STEAKS

PREPARATION TIME 10 MIN

COOKING TIME 15 MIN

SERVINGS 2

INGREDIENTS:

- 1/2 teaspoons garlic powder
- 1 1/2 teaspoons dried basil
- 1 1/2 teaspoons dried oregano
- 1/8 teaspoon salt
- 1/8 teaspoon freshly ground black pepper 4 (4-ounce) top round steaks
- Nonstick cooking spray
- Zest of 1/2 large lemon
- 1 tablespoon fresh lemon juice
- 2 tablespoons crumbled feta cheese

DIRECTIONS:

In a small bowl, mix the garlic powder, basil, oregano, salt, a pepper. Season the steaks on both sides.

Coat the grill grates with cooking spray— Preheat the grill to medium-hi heat (350°F to 400°F).

Grill, the stakes for 6 minutes on each side or until the internal temperature reaches 135°F for medium-rare. Add a few more minutes for medium.

Let the steaks cool, then store them in 4 storage containers. Store the le zest, lemon juice, and feta cheese separately.

To serve, after reheating the steaks, sprinkle with lemon zest and lemon and top with the cheese.

Nutrition: Calories: 180 Total Fat: 3g Total Carbohydrates: 0g Fiber: 0g Sugar: 0g Proteins: 24g

DESSERTS

196. APRICOT & ALMOND CRISP

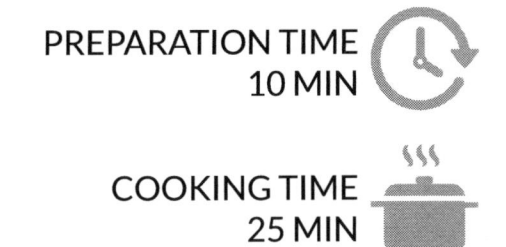

PREPARATION TIME 10 MIN

COOKING TIME 25 MIN

SERVINGS 2

INGREDIENTS:

- 1 teaspoon of olive oil
- 1-pound apricots
- 1/2 cup of almonds
- 1 tablespoon of oats
- 1 teaspoon of anise seeds
- 2 tablespoons of honey

DIRECTIONS:

Remove pits in apricots.

Heat Oven to 350 degrees. Brush olive oil over glass pie dish

Cut apricots and place in pie dish. Sprinkle chopped almonds, oats and anise seeds on top

Drizzle with honey. Bake for 25 minutes.

Serve warm

Nutrition: Calories: 170 Total Fat: 11g Total Carbohydrates: 20g Fiber: 5g Sugar: 10g Protein: 4g

197. FRESH STRAWBERRIES WITH YOGHURT AND HONEY

PREPARATION TIME
5 MIN

COOKING TIME
5 MIN

SERVINGS
2

INGREDIENTS:

- 1 pint of fresh strawberries
- 4 teaspoons honey
- 3 cups of plain low-fat yoghurt
- 4 tablespoons of almonds (toasted and sliced)

DIRECTIONS:

Wash and slice strawberries into quarters

Add 3/4 yoghurt into each serving

Add strawberries to each serving

Top with honey and almonds

Nutrition: Calories: 151 Total Fat: 0.5g Total Carbohydrates: 35g Fiber: 4g Sugar: 30g Protein: 4g

198. FRUIT & NUT BAR

PREPARATION TIME 10 MIN

COOKING TIME 20 MIN

SERVINGS 2

INGREDIENTS:

- 1/2 cup of quinoa flour
- 1/2 cup of oats
- 1/4 cup of flaxseed flour
- 1/4 cup of wheat germ
- 1/4 cup of chopped almonds
- 1/4 cup of chopped dried apricots
- 1/4 cup of chopped dried figs
- 1/4 cup of honey
- 1/4 cup of chopped dried pineapple
- 2 tablespoons of cornstarch

DIRECTIONS:

Heat oven to 300 degrees F.

Place parchment on sheet pan

Mix all the ingredients thoroughly

Pour mixture into pan

Bake for 20 minutes

Cool completely before cutting into pieces

Nutrition: Calories: 109 Total Fat: 2g Total Carbohydrates: 20g Fiber: 0g Sugar: 8g Protein: 1g

199. MILK CHOCOLATE PUDDING

PREPARATION TIME
5 MIN

COOKING TIME
5 MIN

SERVINGS
2

INGREDIENTS:
- 3 tablespoons of cornstarch
- 2 tablespoons of cocoa powder
- 2 tablespoons of sugar
- 1/2 teaspoon of salt
- 2 cups of non-fat milk
- 1/3 cup of chocolate chips
- 1/2 teaspoon of vanilla

DIRECTIONS:

Put cornstarch, cocoa powder, sugar and salt in a saucepan. Mix well.

Whisk in the milk.

Heat over medium flame until thickened.

Take from the heat. Stir in chocolate chips and vanilla until smooth

Pour into a dish and chill

Nutrition: Calories: 120 Total Fat: 3g Total Carbohydrates: 24g Fiber: 1g Sugar: 16g Protein: 1g

200. ORANGE DREAM SMOOTHIE

PREPARATION TIME 5 MIN

COOKING TIME 5 MIN

SERVINGS 2

INGREDIENTS:

- 1 1/2 cup of orange juice
- 1 cup of light vanilla soy milk
- 1/3 cup of silken
- 1 tablespoon of dark honey
- 1 teaspoon of grated orange zest
- 1/2 teaspoon of vanilla extract
- 5 ice cubes
- 4 peeled orange segments

DIRECTIONS:

Blend orange juice, soy milk, silken, honey, vanilla, ice cubes and orange zest

Blend until smooth

Pour into glasses

Garnish with orange segment

Nutrition: Calories: 218 Total Fat: 1g Total Carbohydrates: 24g Fiber: 1g Sugar: 16g Protein: 24g

CONCLUSION

Dash Diet is easy to follow, and a food guide readily available recipes for people who want to lose weight to improve their health. It is designed to lower blood pressure and help you lose weight with no need to count calories. This cookbook has no limitations on portions of food. However, it is important to make the right choices. The dash diet follows a healthy approach. It is meant to help you enjoy a long life.

There's no reason to deal with hypertension, but you will still need any medication prescribed by your doctor even with this dietary change. You'll need to exercise regularly to maintain your health and reap the full benefits. With regular exercise and healthy eating, a dietary approach to stopping hypertension is manageable.

Anyone who wants to lose weight can eat with the dash diet. This diet restricts the intake of salt, fats, and oils. The dash diet is not vegetarian. However, vegetarians can still use this diet. They should avoid dairy and avoid using animal fats. Vegetarians who eat fish should avoid salt and animal fats. The dash diet is very flexible. It shows you how to make great tasting food that you and your family can enjoy.

The main purpose is to help people who have low self-esteem to improve their health and daily life. You will see benefits to your health if you follow this diet and maintain glucose metabolism and avoid obesity.

Exercise and dietary modifications can help in reducing weight and controlling blood pressure. Keeping track of your performance with exercise or physical activity can help you keep motivated for a longer period. Similarly, a dietary record is also helpful in estimating the daily intake and calories consumed per day.

The Dash strategy is a new way to eat — for a living. When you slip a few days off the eating plan, don't let it keep you from reaching your health goals.

Ask yourself why you got off-track.

Get on track again. Here's how: Tell yourself why you've gone off track. Was it drinking at a party? Have you experienced tension at home or work? Find out what started your sidetrack, and then begin the Dash plan again.

Look out for if you tried to do too much at once.

Anyone starting a new lifestyle sometimes tries to change too much at once. Instead, one or two things should be changed at a time. The only way to succeed is, slowly but surely.

Break down the process into small steps.

Not only does this discourage you from having to do too much at once, but it also makes the changes easier. Break complicated objectives into smaller, easier measures, each achievable.

Write it down.

Keep a record of what you eat and what you do. That can help you figure out the issue. The record also allows you to ensure that each food group and physical activity are being enough every day.

You will see a lot of changes in your lifestyle. Your meals, blood pressure, and health will improve. This will help you live a better life, and you will be healthier.

Printed in Great Britain
by Amazon